BROADCAST FROM THE FRONT

Canadian War Museum

Historical Publication Number 11

Editor: John Swettenham, Curator, Historical Resources

The Canadian War Museum, National Museum of Man, National Museums of Canada

Publications in this series by the Canadian War Museum, National Museum of Man, may be obtained from: Marketing Services Division, National Museums of Canada, Ottawa, Ontario.

1 *Canada and the First World War*, by John Swettenham. Canadian War Muscum, Ottawa, 1968.

2 *D-Day*, by John Swettenham. Canadian War Museum, Ottawa, 1969.

3 *Canada and the First World War*, by John Swettenham. Based on the Fiftieth Anniversary Armistice Display at the Canadian War Museum. Ryerson, Toronto, 1969. Illustrated. Paperback edition, McGraw-Hill Ryerson, Toronto, 1973.

4 *Canadian Military Aircraft*, by J. A. Griffin. Queen's Printer, Ottawa, 1969.

5 *The Last War Drum: The North West Campaign of 1885*, by Desmond Morton. Published by Hakkert, Toronto, in cooperation with the Canadian War Museum, 1972.

6 *The Evening of Chivalry*, by John Swettenham. National Museums of Canada, Ottawa, 1972.

7 *Valiant Men: Canada's Victoria Cross and George Cross Winners*, edited by John Swettenham. Hakkert, Toronto, 1973.

8 *Canada Invaded: 1775-1776*, by George F. G. Stanley. Hakkert, Toronto, 1973.

9 *The Canadian General: Sir William Otter*, by Desmond Morton. Hakkert, Toronto, 1974.

10 *Silent Witnesses/Témoins Silencieux*, by Herbert Fairlie Wood and John Swettenham. Hakkert, Toronto, 1974.

BROADCAST FROM THE FRONT

Canadian Radio Overseas in the Second World War

A.E. Powley

Hakkert, Toronto, 1975

Cover design by Helmut Rath

This book has been written and published with the aid of funds provided by the National Museum of Man, National Museums of Canada.

In the writing of this book the inferences drawn and the opinions expressed are those of the author himself, and the National Museums of Canada are in no way responsible for his presentation of the facts as stated.

International Standard Book Number: 0-88866-565-2

Published by A. M. Hakkert Ltd., 554 Spadina Crescent, Toronto, Canada M5S 2J9

Printed and bound in Canada by The Hunter Rose Co.

CONTENTS

PHOTO CREDITS

Numbers indicate order of appearance
(from top to bottom, left to right on each page)
throughout book.

Arthur Holmes: 1-4, 7, 9, 11, 12, 28, 32, 40, 43, 44, 47, 48

Public Archives of Canada: 8, 10, 13, 14, 17-27, 29-31, 34-39, 42, 46,
49, 51, 53-55

Marcel Ouimet: 33, 41, 50, 52

Captured German photos: 15, 16

British Broadcasting Corporation: 6

Imperial War Museum: 45

ACKNOWLEDGEMENTS

I should like to express my thanks first to Robin Woods, the CBC programme archivist, and his staff, for supplying me with dubbings of Overseas Unit broadcasts; next, to Mrs. Lee M. Leah, for transcribing countless miles of audio tape and for her patience in typing manuscript. Many former members of the unit, most particularly Arthur Holmes (who also helped assemble the illustrations), Bob Bowman, Marcel Ouimet, Peter Stursberg, John Kannawin and Lloyd Moore, contributed their own recollections. E. L. Bushnell, who was the head of CBC programmes during the war, allowed me to see his files on the early days of the Overseas Unit. And I am grateful to John Swettenham and Frank McGuire, of the Canadian War Museum, for editorial assistance and the checking of some facts.

PREFACE

This book is about the CBC Overseas Unit. That is to say it is about the Second World War, war correspondents and the Canadian Broadcasting Corporation, which had its men with the Canadian forces in the United Kingdom and Europe from the arrival of the first troop convoy in 1939 to the last shots in 1945. It consists in large part of broadcasts made on the battlefield thirty years and more ago. Radio played a vital role in the reporting of the war, and it was the CBC which, as Canada's national broadcasting agency, undertook the Canadian part of the job.

The book is also a story from the remote antiquity of broadcasting. In a day when we no longer marvel at televised conversations with men on the moon, it is strange to remember what a wonder it was in the 1940's that the sound of a falling bomb or an artillery barrage, or a description of battle, could be put on a record in England or Italy or France one day and heard from coast to coast in Canada the next.

During the Second World War, "broadcasting" meant radio and nothing else. There had been some work in television, notably in England by the BBC, but that was something that had to be put aside when the war began. In 1939, most broadcasting was live and from a studio. The use of recordings on the air was a rarity and generally something to be deprecated. And there was no recording equipment anywhere that would nowadays be called portable, though some studio gear gained the designation "mobile" by being installed in wheeled vehicles of great strength.

The war made the use of recordings respectable; it would have been impracticable to move high-powered transmitting stations about a battlefield, and visionary to expect battles to arrange themselves in accordance with network schedules. The war also stimulated the quest for portability.

Still, up to the end, the most portable piece of equipment to go into use was a spring-wound machine which was cranked up by a handle and could cut a disc of three minutes' duration. It didn't need a technician to run it, and it weighed only ten pounds or so. But it didn't come on the scene until the last year of the war, was in very short supply and was unreliable anyway, as some of our correspondents found to their chagrin when discs that should have been full of terrifying battle sounds, recorded at great personal hazard, turned out to be blank. The tape recorder, that indispensable aid to modern electronic reporting, had not yet made its appearance. Late in the war there were a few wire recorders around, but they went wrong as often as they worked, their sound quality was terrible, and they were used only occasionally and experimentally. Apart from these experiments, all the battle recording of those days was done through the old-fashioned medium of cutting needle on rotating disc.

It was a tricky operation. The CBC managed it, and in doing so let loose, in addition to its year-by-year stream of spoken reports, a million detonations from bomb, shell, cannon and a variety of other projectiles and weapons, to resound through living rooms in Canada, the United States and Britain. In fact, the CBC's reporter-engineer teams in Italy and Northwest Europe were the best-equipped people in the actuality business in any theatre of war. From the early stages of the campaign in Italy, the CBC men had not only portable recording units that could be taken as far forward as a jeep could go, and carried still farther forward by hand if necessary, but also a kind of mother-van, a military vehicle converted into a mobile studio, so completely equipped that in it a broadcaster and engineer could blend a collection of battle sounds and commentary into a feature-length programme ready for the air.

In the job of reporting the war it was the broadcasters who gained the kudos, but their voices would not have got far without the engineers. The engineers' share of the partnership went beyond technical proficiency. Many a fine actuality resulted from an engineer's suggestion, or from his initiative when his broad-caster colleague was elsewhere. The engineers shared the broad-casters' status as correspondents as they shared their risks.

Risk was an undeniable factor. It is a necessary part of a war correspondent's job to stay alive so that he can tell his story. But that necessity has frequently to be weighed against the value of the story, and many a correspondent, whether for the CBC or anybody else, often took his life in his hands for the sake of the job to be done.

Since the ensuing narrative does not, this preface must mention the small band of loyal and competent young Englishwomen, seconded by the BBC and headed first by Edna Cooper and later by Daphne Burrows, who kept the Overseas Unit's office in London going. I should say the unit's succession of offices, because in the time of the Blitz there were several bombings out.

In addition to the reports from the fronts and Britain to be sent on to Canada, there was a constant traffic of other pro-grammes going both ways across the Atlantic. There were always scripts to be typed, studio bookings to be made, and reports to be shepherded through censorship. Our women colleagues were a busy lot, and working under Blitz, blackout, buzz bombs and a score of other inconveniences, they were as much at war as any correspondent at the front.

As to why I am the writer, my job required a close acquaintance with the work of the CBC's front line correspondents; and when I had pieced together an account of the Overseas Unit in the years before I joined it in the spring of 1943, I decided I had a good story.

BROADCAST FROM THE FRONT

1-OVERSEAS

The existence of the CBC Overseas Unit—"CBC recording gear, an observer and an engineer"—was first revealed on December 18, 1939, two days before the first fruit of its labours was broadcast over the National Network of the CBC from London. It was not then called the Overseas Unit, and no-one had any idea that it would send programmes across the Atlantic, with the actual sounds of battle, till the Second World War came to an end in Europe in May of 1945.

The unit had its genesis in haste and secrecy; haste so great that the "observer" left his Toronto apartment for unknown horizons with twenty-five cents in his pocket, and secrecy so great that the official who gave him his instructions was not told what they were about. The instructing official was E. L. Bushnell, the CBC's general supervisor of programmes. The "observer" was Robert Turnbull Bowman, a large, curly-headed and cheerful young man who rejoiced in the title of Supervisor of Actuality Broadcasts. He was well known as a broadcaster throughout Canada, particularly since the visit of King George VI and Queen Elizabeth earlier that year. It was he who had spoken the first words of the first broadcast as the tour began at Quebec, and he had been on the air almost daily from then until it ended at Halifax.

On the evening of December 4, the telephone rang in Bowman's apartment. Answering it, he found himself being addressed in tones of mysterious urgency by Bushnell, who wanted to know

1

where the portable recording equipment was, and how soon Bowman could get to Halifax with it. "Don't ask me why," he said, "because I don't know. How soon can you start?"

Bowman knew his train schedules and thus was aware that there was a train leaving for Halifax in an hour. He was spared much of the labour of packing because most of his clothes were at the laundry, so he had time to put in some long distance calls to arrange for the transfer of equipment to Halifax. When he reached the station, Bushnell was waiting for him, with money for the journey and a further instruction. On reaching Halifax, he was to report to the local military commander, General C. F. Constantine, and give a password, which through someone's playfulness was "Constantinople." At that point he would be told what it was all about.

Two days later the Maritime Express reached Halifax with Bowman on board, and he had no need to ask why he was there. Five famous liners, the *Aquitania*, the *Empress of Britain*, the *Empress of Australia*, the *Duchess of Bedford* and the *Monarch of Bermuda*, were tied up at dockside, and the battleship *Resolution* was out in the stream. Obviously, troops were going overseas. Nevertheless, Bob found General Constantine and gave the password, and was told officially that the 1st Canadian Division was to sail within a few days for a destination that could not be disclosed. His job was to record scenes of the troops boarding their ships, and of the sailing, and from his recordings put together a programme which could be broadcast after the ships had arrived wherever they were going.

Bowman listened with proper respect, said to himself "Nuts to that," and went away to do some quick thinking. It was out of the question to try to say what was in his mind over the regular telephone; the lines were monitored, and the conversation would be cut at the first mention of ships or troops. But he remembered that the army had its own communication system, and by means of this he got a secret message to Gladstone Murray, the general manager of the CBC, in Ottawa. The gist of it was that instead of recording a programme on the dock and waving goodbye to the troops, he ought to sail with them and do his broadcast from the other end of the voyage. Furthermore, he should have an engineer and recording equipment with him so that he could make recordings en route. Gladstone Murray agreed and went into instant action. So another mysterious telephone call brought another hasty flitting. This time the call was to Arthur W. Holmes, a member of the CBC's engineering staff stationed at Windsor, Ontario, and like Bowman a veteran of the recent royal tour. The caller, in Montreal, was J. Alphonse Ouimet, later to be president of the CBC but then its general supervising engineer.

Before he joined the Canadian Radio Broadcasting Commission (the CBC's predecessor) in 1933, Holmes had been in the Merchant Marine. His seafaring career over, he learned flying, and having his pilot's license, volunteered for the Royal Canadian Air Force at the outbreak of war. The offer of a commission had reached him a few days before Ouimet's telephone call, and his application for war service leave from the CBC was on Ouimet's desk. Ouimet asked him if he would be willing to go on an assignment "involving some personal risk".

"I can't tell you what it is," he said, "but I think it will fit in with your plans." Holmes had heard the rumours then current that the 1st Division was going overseas soon.

"Yes, I'll take it," he said.

Ouimet told him he would have to catch the five o'clock train to Toronto, which meant leaving in less than two hours, to make the necessary connections for the east coast. There were only two engineers at the Windsor station, Holmes and Max Gilbert. They alternated on duty shifts. Holmes telephoned Gilbert, told him he had been ordered away in a hurry, and asked him to come in and take over. Gilbert had some distance to travel to the studio, and by the time he got there Holmes was in danger of missing his train.

"Goodbye," Holmes said.

"Yes, but where are you going?" cried Max.

"I don't know," said Arthur as he ran.

And so, getting his orders as he posted eastward, he joined Bowman on board the *Aquitania* on the evening of December 9. The convoy sailed the next morning, carrying General A. G. L. McNaughton and 7,600 officers and men of the 1st Canadian Division. It turned out that great things had hung on Bowman's decision that he must sail with the division. It also turned out that equally great things hung on the choice of Holmes as the engineer to go with him. It was largely through him that the CBC came to excel in broadcasting the sounds of battle. He was to be in many of the Canadians' greatest battles in Europe, and along with two later colleagues, Matthew Halton and Marcel Ouimet, he was to be decorated with the OBE for his services.

The departure that Bowman had been sent to record was recorded instead by J. Frank Willis, already a famous broadcaster in those pioneer days of radio, and destined for even greater fame. The programme went on the air on December 18. It ended with the words:

With those grey ships went CBC recording equipment, an observer and an engineer. A recording in sound of the departure, the crossing and the arrival of the Canadian troops is now in London. Tomorrow night the CBC hopes to bring you a special broadcast by transatlantic beam. This unique departure in wartime news coverage will be heard on the CBC National Network at a time when arrangements have been completed with London.

It was not the next night, but the night after, that the network audience heard Lamont Tilden announce from a Montreal studio: "We take you now to London," and then the transatlantic voice of Bowman: "The First Canadian Division has now arrived in the United Kingdom. Officers and men, safe and sound, every one of them, are now in their training camps."

Calling Bowman's broadcast a "unique departure in wartime news coverage" was justifiable. Wartime news coverage of any kind was unique in December, 1939, and a programme direct from London still a rarity. And there was an additional uniqueness about the programme in its recordings of shipboard activities on the way across. It is Holmes' belief that they were the first recordings ever made at sea. Recording turntables were generally anchored firmly to a studio floor. Cutting records outside the studio was accompanied by elaborate rituals with spirit levels. Apparently no-one had ever thought to see whether a turntable and cutting head would work on a heaving deck.

It had been quite a business getting the equipment aboard ship and in working order. The only equipment designated as "mobile" that the CBC possessed was set up on the pier to record the departure, and the best that could be obtained for the voyage was a standard studio unit, which Holmes set up in the *Aquitania*'s lounge. It required alternating current, and as this wasn't available on board, it had to be provided by a generator, a bulky piece of equipment that weighed 500 pounds and had to be got on board by means of a crane. The equipment being immobile and *Aquitania* a large ship to get around with a microphone, Holmes and Bowman needed a great length of cable. They managed to scrounge this, mostly at the last minute from the mobile unit ashore.

The details that they could tell about the voyage in their broadcast were of course limited by censorship. They were given opportunity to elaborate in a radio programme many years after the war. This from Bowman:

I ran into an unexpected snag before I could sail. When I was taken aboard the *Aquitania* and introduced to the captain, with an explanation of why I was there, there was a mighty blast from this little bulldog of a man who commanded one of the largest ships afloat. "Why damme eyes, sir, there's a war on, and they propose to send a broadcasting man on my ship? Why damme eyes, the answer is no." And I was hustled off in short order. It took high level intervention to get him to change his mind.

Bowman recalled that a couple of days out, the convoy ran into a fog so thick that the *Empress of Britain* nearly put her bow through *Aquitania*'s stern. When the fog lifted, the destroyers were gone and so was the *Empress of Australia*. "We worried about our troops out there all alone, without the battleship to protect her from the *Scharnhorst* and the *Gneisenau*, which we knew to be on the prowl."

A fellow passenger was Gillis Purcell, then General Superintendent and subsequently General Manager of The Canadian Press. The three of them were on deck together one evening when a Royal Navy cruiser stuck her bow over the horizon astern and began flashing a signal to the battleship. Holmes knew Morse. "Funny," he said, "All it says is 'Luke 15:6.'" It was their first acquaintance with the naval habit of using scriptural references for condensing information. They trooped down to the ship's library, looked up the passage and read: "Rejoice with me, for I have found my sheep which was lost."

"So we knew," Bowman said, "that the *Empress of Australia* was safe, and sure enough she joined us next morning and obediently fell into line, although I heard a long time afterwards that the captain of the *Australia* didn't like convoys and there was a suspicion that he'd taken advantage of the fog to slip away and run on his own." That was an incident of the voyage that didn't get into the programme from London, like the ensuing one which Bowman told in that much later broadcast.

On our second last day at sea we woke to find ourselves screened by Royal Navy destroyers which steamed past us in a salute to General McNaughton, and the aircraft carrier *Furious* had taken station at the head of the convoy. This was very comforting, and during the day an Anson aircraft also flew past us in a salute and we could see her crew waving. We went to bed on what was to prove our last night at sea (for we still didn't know where we were or where we were going), when there was a tremendous crash and the huge *Aquitania* heeled over, then righted herself.

We soon learned that we had been in a collision. The passenger liner *Samaria*, outward bound from Liverpool for New York, had come clean through our escort, hell for leather. She had missed our destroyer screen, missed the *Furious* in front, and sideswiped the *Aquitania*. The *Samaria* had to go back to Liverpool, but fortunately we were able to keep going, minus a few lifeboats on the port side. A matter of two or three feet had possibly saved the flagship of the First Canadian Division from being sent to the bottom. That was the second time we had nearly been run down, and during six Atlantic convoys in the first four years of the war I became almost accustomed to it.

And this from Holmes:

The ship was full, but only to her normal passenger complement, which meant that we were having a de luxe crossing. The memory of that first trip was to haunt me for the rest of the war.

I made several crossings during the years that followed, some on small freighters during the worst of the Battle of the Atlantic, under constant attack night and day, watching ships next to us blow up and disappear. Once I sailed on a troopship smaller than the *Aquitania* with five times the number of troops on board, jammed in ten and fifteen to a cabin, and this one was torpedoed and sunk. Each time the memory of the *Aquitania*, the gaiety of the First Contingent and the odd illusions we had at that time about war, would come back and it would seem like a dream of many years ago.

One happy result of the relaxed atmosphere of the voyage was that the officers of the Royal 22nd Regiment were able to give a cocktail party in one of the *Aquitania*'s so-far unconverted large salons. Bowman and Holmes, who had hit it off well with the regiment from the start, were invited, and thereafter, when the troops were in camp, they were regular guests at the Van Doos' mess parties. Among the notable people whom Holmes met at some of them were General de Gaulle and the Duke of Gloucester.

Bowman's account of the crossing concluded:

Some things are hazy now. I remember getting off the *Aquitania* and going ashore in a small boat, and wandering around in the pitch dark of a blackout. I remember arriving at the Piccadilly Hotel in London and wondering where Art Holmes was and how we would ever meet again to get our recordings on the air. [Holmes, of course, had stayed behind until he could get the equipment and recordings off the ship, with that precise object in mind.] But we did eventually meet somehow, and went to the BBC, only to find that they recorded everything at 78 r.p.m. while we recorded at 33. What with this seemingly insuperable difficulty, and censors, how we got our story on the air is something of a miracle.

The miracle achieved, Bowman was able to announce at the programme's end that others would follow. The CBC, having to its surprise shipped two of its men overseas, had decided to keep them there for a time while it made up its mind what to do with them. The two men had already made up their minds. The 1st Division was to join the British Expeditionary Force in France as soon as its training was complete, and they meant to be there with it. They were given an office and studio facilities at Broadcasting House by the BBC, who were to be the Overseas Unit's willing and helpful hosts throughout the war. Whenever the unit was bombed out, they always found it new quarters.

Their initial programme out of the way, Bowman and Holmes set off on visits to the Canadians' training areas, lugging along the equipment they had used on board the *Aquitania*, to record everything they could of camp life, for home consumption in a programme they called "With the Troops in England." It was a hit from the start.

One of Bowman's difficulties was to persuade Canadian Military Headquarters in London that radio could cover news and special events. The officer in charge of public relations at CMHQ —incidentally a staunch ally of the CBC throughout the war—at first had a rather limited view of radio's capabilities. When Bowman protested about not having been told in advance of such things as a visit by the King and Queen to a Canadian regiment, he would answer: "Well, what could you do?" So Bowman took his troubles to General McNaughton. He tells the sequel.

A few days later there was a parade on the grounds of a country estate. McNaughton was taking the salute, or commanding the parade, or something. I had the recording gear on the upper balcony of the mansion looking down on the parade. Everything was in readiness when the General shouted: "Are you ready, Bowman?" I replied that I was. Then, and only then, did the parade start. I had no more trouble at CMHQ.

One of the most popular features of "With the Troops in England" was the "Messages Home" section, in which the troops recorded brief greetings to parents, brothers and sisters, wives and sweethearts. It got into the programme by accident. A Canadian soldiers' canteen was being opened at British Columbia House in London, and Bowman had somewhat ambitiously booked half an hour of network time for a live broadcast of the event in Canada by transatlantic beam. He hoped the speeches would be over in time for him to get them all in. To his horror they were all over in ten minutes, and he found himself facing twenty minutes of air time with nothing to put in it. But deliverance appeared in the instant of black realization, in the form of the canteen's first customer, across the counter from him at the head of a line of soldiers pushing their trays along the cafeteria rails. Inspiration seized him. "Would you like to send a message to the folks at home?" he asked, and handed the microphone over. The soldier would, and did, and so did the men following him, until the twenty minutes were filled.

Bowman's main feeling at the time was one of relief. But during the next few days he was swamped with cables from appreciative parents. One said simply: "Bless you. Tonight I heard my son." It dawned on him that he had discovered a need, and thereafter, all his troop programmes included some messages home.

The recording equipment they had brought from Canada was mobile only by muscle power and necessity. It travelled between the BBC and the camps by hired van, and to various London rendezvous by taxi. Fortunately there were left in London at that time a few antique and oversized taxis into which it could be coaxed. Something better was needed, and it was with that in mind that, shortly before Bowman's discovery of the "messages home" idea, Arthur Holmes went to France for a look at the front and the stimulation of ideas on the kind of equipment needed for covering a war.

"We decided," Holmes related in that much later radio programme,

that I should make a trip to the front line covered by British troops, and the Maginot Line of the French. A request was made through Canada House, and early in January, 1940, I was called down to Whitehall and eventually had several papers issued to me. These included a white permit from the British Army and a safe conduct pass from the French. I was told that in about a week or ten days I would be notified where to meet a conducting officer, and the trip to BEF headquarters would begin.

In my ignorance of army red tape this part did not mean much to me; neither did the fact that they eluded the question of where the headquarters were located when I asked. However, that evening I dropped into a pub in Leicester Square, and the barmaid happened to mention that her boy friend was stationed at BEF headquarters in Arras. This information was enough for me, and next morning I left for Dover, crossed to France, and by various means, including hitch-hiking, made my way towards Arras.

I was in civilian clothes, and I noticed that as I got closer to the front I was being regarded with some suspicion. This did not bother me, but soon after I entered Arras I was picked up by a British patrol, and eventually landed before the commanding officer.

He agreed that my papers were all right, but said I was supposed to be with a party arriving in another week, and anyway, how had I found out where the BEF headquarters were? The reaction was startling, to say the least, when I informed him that a barmaid in London had told me, but when everything came down to earth again

I was assigned to quarters, and one of the officers invited me out for a drink.

I discovered later that this wasn't just courtesy, as when I got back to my room all my possessions had been thoroughly searched, and it was apparent that even the lining in my coat had been removed. They also communicated with London, and later that night I was cleared, and of course, every courtesy was offered me for the rest of my stay at the front.

Next day I went up to a section of the Maginot Line. We could see German soldiers standing by the bank of a river about two hundred yards away. I asked a French officer why they weren't shot down. He said they didn't want to start any trouble, and that both sides behaved in this fashion.

Next he was taken to the British front. The troops were in trenches, after the manner of the First World War. In front of the trenches was a ditch, which they told him was a tank trap. It struck him as inadequate. For defence against tanks they had, as far as he could see, only anti-tank rifles.

"What are you going to do if the Germans attack?" he asked the officer who was showing him around.

"Oh, we'll stop 'em," he was told.

It was depressing, but somehow the idea germinated. The war was not going to be fought from the Maginot Line or from a line of British trenches. He suspected that when the fighting came, it was going to be a war of manoeuvre and movement. The CBC was going to need equipment that could move with it. He got back to London as quickly as he could and immediately put in his application for passage to Canada. He was on board ship at Liverpool, bound for Halifax, before January was out.

The core of his idea was the value of sound, and the ability of the microphone to capture it. So the equipment must be capable of producing anything from a straight voice report to the whole sound spectrum of battle. Clearly, the first thing needed was some sort of vehicle carrying plenty of recording equipment and its own power supply, big enough to be put to use as a wheeled studio, and mobile enough to get close to the battle zone. Something more mobile still would have to come next: perhaps gear that a correspondent could carry right into the battle. But the vehicle must come first.

It was easier dreamed of than found. At the beginning of 1940, Canadian factories were just tooling up for war production, and there was no stream of military vehicles coming off assembly lines. But in the Ford plant at Windsor Holmes found the chassis for a vehicle that was to become a regimental aid post, a sort of forward area hospital on wheels. A vehicle of that size would make a positively de luxe wheeled studio. He ordered one, to be built to his specifications. Then he hurried back to Montreal, where the CBC's Engineering Headquarters could turn its resources to the job of devising and building the equipment to go into the vehicle.

Meanwhile, the CBC being thus in the process of committing itself to battle, its programme head, E. L. Bushnell, took ship for England to make some necessary arrangements. Looking back, the corporation seems from then on to have displayed a grand nonchalance in the way it moved its people back and forth through the Battle of the Atlantic.

To begin with, there would have to be two reporters with the troops, one each for the English and French networks, and an engineer to go with them. That meant three front line accreditations. There would have to be someone to take Bowman's place in England when he went to France. Bushnell got to London on March 8. Since the Canadians' move was then expected about May 1, there was no time to lose.

He and Bowman went to see General McNaughton. The general welcomed the idea of having CBC correspondents with his division, but the trouble was that the matter of accreditation rested with the War Office, and the War Office, apparently still nursing its First World War aversion for war correspondents, was already in process of turning down an application made through Canadian Military Headquarters. It was clearly a case needing high level intervention, so next day they went to Canada House to see the High Commissioner, Vincent Massey, and his assistant, Lester B. Pearson. The interview was a success. They were advised to apply for accreditation to the British Expeditionary Force, which would give our men the run of the whole British-Canadian front. Further, if Bushnell would make a written request, the High Commissioner himself would make the necessary application to the War Office. So that was taken care of.

Arrangements were already under way for plentiful air time in the BBC's short wave service for transmitting broadcasts from the United Kingdom to Canada. There was now the matter of transmission from France, no-one then dreaming that France would shortly be occupied by the enemy. So off went Bushnell and Bowman to Paris and the Canadian Legation there. Their first call was on the Second Secretary, whose name was Pierre Dupuy, and their next on the Minister, Colonel Georges Vanier. With the minister's blessing, Mr. Dupuy introduced them to the appropriate French broadcasting officials, and in no time at all they had the assurance of all the short wave broadcasting time the CBC might need. They flew back to London in triumph, at the Easter weekend. They would doubtless have felt even better if they could have known that of the four men whose aid they had invoked and received, two would become governors general of Canada, one a prime minister, and the fourth an ambassador and the Commissioner General of Expo '67.

There remained the matter of getting the new men and Holmes' recording van across the Atlantic in time. Three volunteers were standing by in Montreal: the already well-known Gerard Arthur, who was to be the French Network's correspondent; Albert E. Altherr, an engineer with impressive professional qualifications and a linguist; and Gerry Wilmot, an announcer who knew the entertainment business and whose voice, whether as news reader or as concert compère, was to become familiar to every Canadian in the overseas forces. He was to look after the work in the United Kingdom. The way was now clear for them to sail, and Bushnell was happy at getting word that they would leave Canada on April 10. He was not so happy to learn that the recording van could not be shipped before May 1. His latest word on the Canadians' move to France was that it had been postponed a couple of weeks to May 15. That was cutting things too fine.

There was a minor complication. Thanks to Mr. Massey, the War Office was willing to issue the accreditations, but the War Office wanted things done properly. The correspondents' application forms must be signed by the CBC's general manager, Gladstone Murray, and he was in Canada. And time was short and transatlantic mail uncertain. Luckily General Victor Odlum, who had just been appointed to command the 2nd Canadian Division, arrived in London at about the same time as the CBC trio from Montreal. The general also happened to be vice-chairman of the CBC Board of Governors, so he signed the forms.

Hope sprang eternal in those days. Word came that the 1st Division's move was further postponed to June 1, and that meant that the recording van would be in time. But from some quarter or other came a warning to cloud Bushnell's optimism. "With the possibility of new theatres of war opening up," he wrote, "there is of course no guarantee that the First Division will go to France. I have been given to understand on good authority that General McNaughton is desirous of keeping his division intact. Even if they do not go to France it is likely that wherever they go it will be as a unit. Such being the case, our staff will accompany them, but there is the possibility of our not being able to arrange to get programmes out of the country."

He finished his report on board ship for home. Near the end, it said: "Mr. Bowman, Mr. Arthur and Mr. Altherr were fitted for their uniforms before I left. I have arranged with the BBC to pay the bill and invoice the CBC."

Bushnell got back to Canada on May 12. Two days earlier, the Germans had invaded Holland, Belgium and Luxembourg. On May 15 the Dutch army capitulated, and on May 28 the Belgian army followed suit. The evacuation of the British Expeditionary Force from the Dunkirk beaches was complete by June 4. The gentlemen in England, newly arrayed, would have nowhere else to wear their uniforms for a long time to come.

2–BLITZ

Still, they were lovely uniforms.

The CBC had never had any war correspondents before, and had no idea how they should be dressed. It had to seek official advice. Goodness knows where the ensuing directive came from, but it looked like the issue of some corner of the War Office that hadn't caught up on its wars. The wardrobe of a war correspondent was to include a "British warm," the stylish short overcoat worn by officers of field rank and upwards in the 1914-18 war, and riding boots and breeches. The fittings at Burberry's in the Haymarket were solemn rituals. The cut and fit of the breeches had to be tested on a wooden horse that had been bestridden for that purpose by generations of cavalry officers including, according to what one of our men was told, the great Duke of Wellington himself.

The finery was sometimes embarrassing. It was apt to draw salutes from colonels not quite sure what magnificence was approaching. Bowman bravely persisted in full fig for a time for occasions like troop reviews and interviews with important people, and when, later on, Holmes found a livery stable on Wimbledon Common and undertook to teach his colleague to ride, the two of them found appropriate use for their breeches and boots. It was merely incidental that Wimbledon Common was full of unexploded bombs from enemy aircraft. Now and then one went off while they rode, and Bowman's horse would bolt. But the day was to come when all the breeches and tall boots and British warms would be stored away in steamer trunks, to be taken home as souvenirs after the war.

Holmes got back to England about the time Bushnell reached Canada; in time to hear Churchill's "blood, toil, tears and sweat" speech of May 13 and thus with a few days to spare before going down to Tilbury docks to see his recording van unloaded. It was a huge vehicle, and when he had driven it up to London and parked beside Broadcasting House, the office girls who came down to admire it named it "Big Betsy" at sight. There was nothing like Betsy in all England. She contained three turntables, which meant that one could go on recording without interruption for as long as one wanted, and she had playback equipment. One could dub from disc to disc, edit, and in fact produce a finished programme, ready to be fed into the short wave transmitters, without leaving her spacious interior. Intended for the battle-fields of France, Betsy never got there. But she was to become a heroine of the Blitz, and accumulate a collection of shrapnel scars unmatched by any of the vehicles that followed her and did get into battle.

Meanwhile there was lots for her to do. More troops were constantly being landed in England, which meant more camps to visit and more Canadian troop programmes to go on the air, and there was plenty of other work at hand. She had barely put in her first appearance in the vicinity of Broadcasting House when word of her extraordinary recording capability reached the Air Ministry, which requested her help in the training of aircraft spotters.

A big part of Britain's air defence was played by the ground spotters whose job it was to detect the approach of enemy air-craft with the aid of big sound dishes that looked like oversized parabolic microphones. The trouble at that time was that in most of England nobody had yet heard an enemy plane. But a few enemy planes were coming over, and their sound was recogniz-able enough because the pilots de-synchronized their engines as they approached the coast, to make the sound harder to pinpoint. So by official request, Holmes and Bert Altherr each made a few sorties in Betsy towards the south coast, and between them recorded all the enemy aircraft engine sound needed to instruct the ground spotters all over England.

Betsy became a familiar sight as she parked—doubtless to the frequent discommoding of traffic—in various streets of London's West End for recording sessions with great officers of state and other notabilities. Bowman is the author of these two reminiscences.

Art Holmes and I had a fascinating experience when Lord Beaverbrook was Minister of Aircraft Production. He had agreed to do a special broadcast for Canada, so we drove the mobile unit to his office in the Shell Building on the Strand. Art parked the van in front while I took an armful of microphone cord and a microphone upstairs to Beaverbrook's offices. His secretary met me, and warned me again and again not to waste Beaverbrook's time: to get the interview over as quickly as possible because "you know how busy he is."

Finally the moment came when I was admitted to Beaverbrook's office. He was sitting at his desk with about six telephones in front of him, and kept calling or answering people on most of them while I stood behind his chair. He never looked at me, or said a word to me, but after ten minutes, perhaps, suddenly said: "Are you ready, Bowman?" I put the microphone in front of him, and said down the line to Art, "Start recording ten seconds from now." Then I told Beaverbrook to go ahead, which he did. When he finished I grabbed the microphone and headed for the door, but as I was backing out, wrapping up cord as I went, I had a hunch and said: "I know how busy you are, Lord Beaverbrook, but would you like to hear the recording played back to you?" For the first time he looked up, and said: "Why, yes, I would." So I explained that it would be necessary to come down to our recording van to hear it. That didn't worry him a bit. He put on his hat and coat, and the war effort stopped while we went down the elevator together, and out on the street where our van was parked. I helped Beaverbrook into the van, and said: "This is Art Holmes, sir, our chief engineer," and to Art I said: "Lord Beaverbrook would like to have that recording played back to him." In his best Detroit voice, Art said: "Well sit down there, and don't shake the van.

Beaverbrook sat down like a lamb, and obviously revelled in hearing his own voice on our equipment, which was the best thing of its kind at that time. When it was over he congratulated us, and said: "Is there anything I can do for you, Bowman?" I replied, "Yes, sir, there is. We'd like to take recording equipment on a bombing raid over Germany. We've been to the Air Ministry, and to the RAF, but they won't let us go. Could you help us?" Beaverbrook replied: "I'll fix it." We're still waiting.

In those days Leslie Howard did a weekly broadcast which was sent to the USA, and our equipment was so good that the BBC asked if we would go to his home in the country and record it. This was a real treat. Art and I would drive to the Howards' lovely country place every Sunday, have lunch with the family, and then record his 15-minute programme.

One day I asked Leslie Howard if he would let us record a special programme for the CBC, a sort of "The Leslie Howards at Home," and he agreed. So after lunch, before he did his programme for the USA, he rehearsed the family, what he would do, and what they would say. I just gave him the microphone, and he waltzed around the room giving instructions. Thinking back on it his performance was very much like Danny Kaye's today. However, before I gave him the microphone I had whispered to Art down the line: "Record the rehearsal.

When Leslie had finished the rehearsal, he said to me: "I think we're ready to record," and I said: "It's all right, Mr. Howard, we have it all now." There was great laughter, and Leslie Howard enjoyed it as much as any of us. When we played the record back, the whole family was in stitches, and his daughter said to him: "Now, daddy, you can see how officious you are." That was the programme we used, with his permission.

There was one time when Betsy parked behind the garden wall of No. 10 Downing Street while Winston Churchill recorded an address for broadcast in Canada. That recording session afforded Holmes an encounter that he found as impressive as the one when he turned up unexpectedly at BEF Headquarters in Arras.

Bowman was away on one of his transatlantic jaunts, and the microphone was being handled by Rooney Pelletier, a recent addition to the Overseas Unit. The arrangement was that Pelletier would bring the microphone and cord back to the van when the recording was over. The recording ended, but Pelletier didn't return. After a due period of waiting, Holmes went in search. Following the microphone cord, he pushed open a door and found himself face to face with Churchill across a large table in a large room. Churchill looked startled. He was alone when Arthur came through the door, but almost immediately a large man, with "bodyguard" written all over him, materialized through another door. The two stared. Holmes, feeling that conversation was required, said: "I was looking for Rooney."

"Oh," said Churchill, relaxing, "he left half an hour ago."

Betsy got her first taste of war in the Battle of Britain, when Holmes used to take her cruising between London and the south coast, in what time he could spare from other chores, to record the sounds of dogfights high above. "The Battle of Britain" was the name that Churchill coined in advance of Germany's attempt to knock out Britain's air defences as the necessary prelude to a seaborne invasion. It began on August 8, 1940, and was over by October, thanks to the "few." But it overlapped and was succeeded by the Blitz—the German attempt to knock England out by massive and continuous bombing of London and her other principal centres of population. Its starting date—although there had already been heavy air raids on other cities—was September 7, when in the afternoon and again at night, London was heavily bombed. From that date onward, London was bombed every night for fifty-seven nights. Its first raid-free night was that of November 3. The bombing went on, heavily and often, for the next six months, during which time the German air force also made large-scale attacks on other cities, beginning with the near demolition of Coventry on November 14 and thereafter ranging the country, with particular attention to ports and manufacturing centres, from Portsmouth and Southampton on the south coast to Liverpool, Belfast and the Clyde. In April 1941, London suffered two exceptionally heavy and destructive raids, which Londoners called "The Wednesday" and "The Saturday," and then, after lesser intervening attacks, two more great raids on the nights of May 10-11 and 13-14. These two raids are considered to mark the end of the Blitz, which left more than 40,000 British civilians killed—20,000 of them in London—and a far greater number wounded.

Holmes' response to the Blitz was characteristic. He was passionately addicted to the recording of sound. He had a mobile studio in which he could record continuously all night if he wanted to. And that was what he made a practice of doing. When the sensible thing to do was head for the nearest bomb shelter, Art instead would head out into the night, to Hyde Park or Regent's Park if the West End was catching it, or else as close

Members of first contingent aboard *Aquitania*

Bowman, Holmes and Betsy, the first CBC recording unit

Bowman discusses broadcast
with Gen. A. G. L. McNaughto[n]

Holmes and Bowman in
the first uniforms

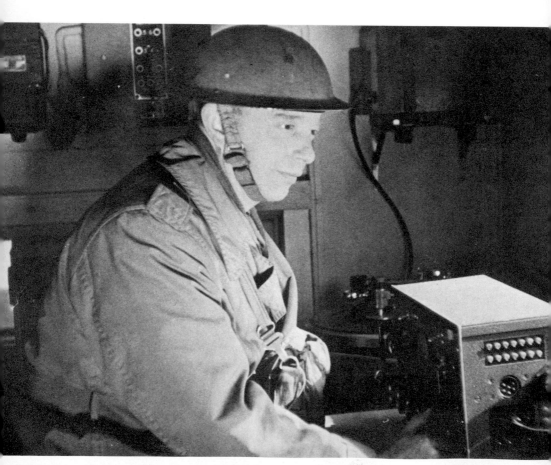

Holmes in the recording van during the London Blitz

King Haakon of
Norway broadcasts

Gen. A. G. L.
McNaughton at
microphone

erry Wilmot

A. E. Powley

Eddie Baudry

Broadcasting House after a bombing

A BBC vehicle in the remains of a CBC office

Bill Herbert (right) chats with RCAF Typhoon pilots

"There goes Bowman" behind shell splashes at Dieppe

The beach at Dieppe

Germans burying Canadian dead after Dieppe

Andrew Cowan

John Kannawin

Clifford Speer

Don Fairbairn (left) and RCAF officer in Normandy

Harold Wadsworth (left) and Ray Mackness before take-off

An English road jammed during Exercise Spartan

Art Holmes (left) with Lloyd Moore leaving for Italy

as he could get to where the bombing seemed to be making the most noise. And he would sit for hours listening through his headphones and cutting disc after disc while the bombs fell.

It didn't strike him as particularly dangerous, because he reckoned that the odds against a direct hit were long. The only thing that did worry him was the shrapnel from our own guns. It spread widely when the shells burst, and he was a bit afraid sometimes that a large and lethal piece would come tearing through the roof or side of the van. That never happened, although Betsy frequently took a peppering, and accumulated a fine collection of shrapnel scars. The end result of his nightly vigils was the finest collection of Blitz sounds that anyone possessed. He made up an album of the best of them, and presented it to the BBC. A dubbing somehow got thence into the hands of the movie industry, and just about every subsequent British war film had some of Holmes' recordings on its sound track—without credit.

Bowman missed the first weeks of the Blitz through being away on naval assignment. He had a lot of friends in the Navy by then. In May, when France was collapsing, the BEF in retreat towards Dunkirk and Britain face to face with invasion, the Royal Canadian Navy had rushed most of its destroyer force across the Atlantic to help defend the British coasts. At once they were very busy patrolling the Channel, fighting German submarines and E boats, and helping to bring off small groups of soldiers and civilians who gathered at various points along the French coast. In the destroyers' brief periods in port, Bowman and Holmes used to visit them to record stories of their exploits. Also, Bowman managed to put in some sea time in fishing trawlers serving as minesweepers in the Channel. So when in August the destroyer *Restigouche* was ordered home to Halifax to refit, the navy invited him to sail in her, record interviews on the way, and broadcast her story to Canada at the end of the voyage.

Restigouche's record was especially distinguished. Soon after arriving in British waters she had gone with her sister ship *St. Laurent* and a British destroyer to the vicinity of St. Valéry-en-Caux, near Dieppe, to help take off some thousands of men of the 51st Highland Division. The Highlanders declined to be taken off until it was too late and German artillery had reached the coast and started shooting at the warships. *Restigouche* took a few shots of her own at the German gunners before withdrawing.

The second day after France's formal surrender found *Restigouche* far down the coast at the foot of the Bay of Biscay, off the small port of St. Jean-de-Luz, which was one of the last escape points to remain open. Off St. Jean-de-Luz, on the previous day, the Canadian destroyer *Fraser* had picked up the Canadian minister to France, Colonel Vanier, and the British ambassador, from the sardine boat in which they had put to sea. Having transferred her passengers to a British cruiser, *Fraser* joined *Restigouche*, and for the next forty-eight hours the two destroyers were at work in the harbour of St. Jean-de-Luz, speeding up the loading, into a mixed fleet that ranged from passenger liners to pleasure boats, of the last of the escaping civilians and troops. The rescue was complete but German guns were firing at them when they cleared the harbour.

Fraser was sunk on the way back to England when she collided with the British cruiser *Calcutta*. By heroic work in the darkness of night, *Restigouche* rescued the greater part of *Fraser*'s company. Back in British waters, *Restigouche* went immediately to work, with two companion Canadian destroyers and a varied host of British ships, at the task of guarding incoming convoys through the southwestern approaches—a convoy route that soon had to be abandoned—under constant attack from submarines and bombers. She was at this work when ordered home. In his official history *The Far Distant Ships*, Joseph Schull writes of her record to this time:

Since the beginning of the war she had steamed 26,181 miles, and fought off a score of air and submarine attacks. She bore the scars of shell fragments from German field guns; and she had acted as senior officer of escort for 242 merchant vessels, none of which had been lost to the enemy.

That was the story that Bowman was invited to tell. Taking with him a recording unit borrowed from the van Betsy, and his engineer colleague Bert Altherr, he reached Liverpool and *Restigouche* as she was preparing to sail.

The following from Bowman:

Bert Altherr and I joined the ship late one afternoon, and that night there were two parties on board. The captain, Commander Horatio Nelson Lay, had some guests in his sea cabin, while two other officers Lieutenant Debbie Piers [later Admiral] and Lieutenant David Groos [later M.P. for Victoria] entertained other guests in the wardroom. These were people who had entertained them in Liverpool. During the evening the Germans put on an air raid. The guests could not go home, so Commander Lay brought his guests to the wardroom and the two parties joined. Piers and Groos were very good at leading sing-songs, so we roared away to the accompaniment of bombs and gunfire, and a good time was had by all. Bert and I recorded the songs and played them back, and I think we eventually gave the recordings to the ship.

The voyage over and the broadcast made, Bowman found himself the guest of honour at a luncheon in Ottawa. The host, a naval officer, made a speech in which he said he had received a glowing report from *Restigouche*'s captain. During a heavy air raid, Bob had "helped avert a possible panic among the ship's guests." Wondering momentarily if he was going to get a medal, Bowman blurted a graceful acknowledgment: "We were all drunk and having a good time."

The *Restigouche* programme aired, Bowman hurried back to England by the first ship available, which was an American freighter sailing from New York. The United States being neutral, he crossed the border in civilian clothes. The US customs men closed his suitcase in a hurry when they saw his uniform inside. On board, he found that the freighter was loaded to the gunwales with machine guns and rifles, part of the stream of weapons which the United States was pouring across the Atlantic to rearm the British Army after Dunkirk.

Meanwhile, two somewhat similarly explosive events had happened in London: the start of the bombing and the return of E. L. Bushnell. Bush had made a deep impression at the higher levels of the BBC by the way he stormed through official barriers when he was over to clear the way to France for his correspondents and to get an unimaginable amount of British air time devoted to programmes from Canada for the Canadian forces in Britain. The BBC had decided that he was just the man they needed to run the North American Service, the most important of their overseas services since its job was to publicize and win sympathy for the Commonwealth war effort in the United States. So they had borrowed him from the CBC.

Bushnell got to London on August 16 and reported immediately to Broadcasting House. He had been there barely an hour when the air raid sirens sounded. Some of the very senior officials gathered in the council chamber to give him a welcoming party remarked that while they knew he was an emphatic man, this did seem to be overdoing things a bit.

Bushnell's presence in London resolved a frustration for Arthur Holmes in the early days of the Blitz. With his fellow sound enthusiast Bowman away, there was nobody in the office to be interested in the programme value of his bomb recordings, and the pile of discs on his desk grew unheeded—until one day Bushnell paid him a visit and made a request in language that for him was extraordinarily diffident. For all his fire, he did not like asking people to risk their lives, and he was unaware of Holmes' affinity for air raids. Would it be possible, he wondered, for Art to record a few air raid sounds, so that he could let the people of North America hear what the Blitz was like? Arthur led him to the recordings on his desk. Thereafter, the sounds of Blitz echoed regularly through North American households.

One of Arthur Holmes' regular duties was a monthly report to Alphonse Ouimet at Engineering Headquarters in Montreal. He had a way of putting things. Thus, on September 8, in a report for August delayed by bombing: "For a moment last night I thought the CBC were going to be minus a van as a dive bomber came straight down at it, passed over at about a hundred feet, but fortunately didn't drop anything there."

The report for September was equally laconic.

Recordings amounted to 172. This is less than for the previous month because of a standby period of about seven days when an invasion was expected and it was thought best to keep the van standing by in London. Since then however several trips to camp have been made and concerts recorded for the new Saturday night series of troop concerts for the CBC. . . .

During air raids, which start at about eight o'clock each night and continue through until morning, it is compulsory to drive with only very dim parking lights. Under these conditions damage to the truck is to be expected through collision or side-swiping. . . .

On September 4 a sound effects record of bombs dropping was made, and two later records of anti-aircraft guns and more bombs dropping were added to the collection. The first record was made at very close range and a good effect produced.

Holmes' faith in the odds against a direct hit led him to undertake another job. A number of underground railway stations in the poor districts of London's East End were so deep as to be ideal bomb shelters, and bunks were built in tiers along the platforms. To brighten things up, producers from the BBC would now and then descend to the depths and conduct sing-songs. A lot of people in the BBC had cast envious eyes on Big Betsy and her recording capability, and it occurred to someone there that she would be ideal for recording some of these sing-songs so that they could be subsequently edited down to programme length and broadcast.

Would Arthur oblige? Arthur would. So, having loaded up with enough microphone cable to penetrate the deepest Underground, he would drive on the designated evening to the designated station, descend—trailing cable behind him—set up microphones, then go back to the van and sit recording the concert going on below while bombs and shrapnel descended from above. When the concert was over he would go down to the safe depths, retrieve his microphones and cable, return to the surface and drive back to Broadcasting House, whether or not the raid was still on.

The Blitz made the weekly camp visits a relief. A night in the country, away from the bombing, was something to be valued. But there always came the time when, after a day spent putting the programme together on Big Betsy's turntables, some one had to take it back to London that evening for broadcast to Canada. Holmes would later recall with a certain gloom: "It generally turned out to be me." It would be dark, and the attack would have begun, by the time the van reached the outskirts of London. A heavy raid invariably meant traffic diversions because of burst water or gas mains, collapsed buildings or cratered roadways. The darkness of a blackout has to be experienced to be understood, and unless there were fires to illuminate the scene, the driver's only light was the exiguous gleam from narrow slits in otherwise blacked-out headlamps. So by tortuous and unfamiliar ways, the night full of gunfire and the howling of bombs, and the earth shuddering with explosions, the van would make its slow way through London's approaches to the West End and the BBC. But no edition of "With the Troops in England" was ever cancelled because of an air raid.

The returned Bowman, with Holmes, missed death by about twenty minutes in the Overseas Unit's second bombing-out. The first had been earlier in the Blitz. The CBC needing more space than the single office originally allotted to it in Broadcasting House, the BBC had found it for them in one of its adjacent buildings in Langham Street. A direct hit demolished that building one night when no-one was in it, so the BBC somehow found new space back in the already over-crowded Broadcasting House. Times were trying enough there. Photographs taken during the Blitz show how hard the Germans were trying to put the BBC out of business. Broadcasting House itself, the prime target, stood like a battered Rock of Gibraltar with ruin all around. Close about it, whether you looked north, south, east or west, you looked at the rubble piles left by near misses.

On the night of the second bombing-out, Bowman and Holmes got back to London late from an expedition to the south coast, where they had gone in the van in the hope of recording a bombardment from the German cross-Channel guns. A heavy air raid was going on when they reached London, and they drove towards the West End with parachute flares and bomb explosions all around. No-one was allowed in the building during a raid, but they had been away a few days and wanted to get their mail. So they managed to slip by the security guards, went up to the offices, picked up their letters and, again successfully eluding the guards, got outside and drove off. Twenty minutes later a parachute mine floated down and hit Broadcasting House. It wrecked a lot of the building, the CBC's new premises included. One's sense of proportion is apt, happily, to bend somewhat in accommodation with extraordinary circumstances, and Bowman's principal feeling about the destruction of his office was regret over the loss of the silver cigarette case that had been presented to him for his part in broadcasting the 1939 Royal Tour.

The Overseas Unit had to be moved again, this time with a number of similarly bombed-out people, to a taken-over girls' school in Regent's Park. It was a brief tenancy, for within a few weeks the school was destroyed by incendiary bombs. After this, the unit was moved to a large building, already blitzed and rebuilt, at 200 Oxford Street, within a stone's throw of Oxford Circus. It was handy to Broadcasting House, had a tube station just across the street and half the bus routes in London practically passing its door, and was within easy walking distance of Canadian Military Headquarters, Whitehall and Westminster. And although there was one subsequent move, just around the corner to 32 Great Castle Street, it was not the result of enemy action. The Germans went on bombing London, but they had lost the knack of hitting the BBC.

One astonishing result of the coincidence of Bushnell and the Blitz was the introduction of Britain to soap opera. The great fire raid of December 29, 1940, may have had something to do with it. He was sharing a flat with Bowman at the time. Having heard the alert and the opening of the barrage, they sat down calmly enough to dinner. When they had finished, they went down to the street to see how things were going, and were surprised to see the sky lit by flames. Thereupon they climbed up the fire escape to the roof, and were even more surprised. The whole square mile of the City, to the east, seemed to be in flames. So they telephoned Arthur Holmes, a near neighbour, and asked him to get a car and drive them to where they could get a closer look.

When Holmes picked them up the fighters had chased the raiders off and the gunfire had stopped, but the fires raged on. They left the car in the Haymarket and walked through Trafalgar Square, along the Strand, then towards the river and along the Embankment to Blackfriars Bridge. A pall of smoke lit by a lurid glow hung over them. Underfoot thousands of feet of fire hose lay everywhere, "looking like snakes that had crawled out of the river," Bushnell said in a broadcast when he was back in Canada a few months later. Dozens of fire engines roared by them. They saw the dome of St. Paul's silhouetted against the flames, and other churches that were completely burned out. And they chatted with firemen and some of the hundreds of bystanders. Bushnell was especially impressed by one old woman who kept running out of her basement doorway with cups of tea for the firemen. He wondered how she could manage it, with tea rationed. A few months later, "Front Line Family" was born.

Bushnell thought how effective, in the terms of his job of publicizing the British war effort in the United States, a radio serial about the everyday doings of an ordinary family in extraordinary times could be. To explain his idea to the BBC he had some sample soap opera recordings sent over. Those who heard them were impressed. There was an initial difficulty in finding a playwright; the genre was foreign to British writers. Then Bushnell met Alan Melville, working at that time for the BBC and destined for a tremendously successful post-war career. He took Melville to dinner at the Café Royal, where all playwrights seemed to dine during the war, and expounded his idea. An air raid was in progress while they talked, and his persuasions were reinforced by frequent bomb explosions near by. Out of that dinner conversation was born the British Family Robinson, whose daily joys and sorrows in the common struggle were to be heard over hundreds of radio stations in the United States and Canada —and in farther distant places—in the serial "Front Line Family."

Bushnell's idea was that the cast of characters should be members of an ordinary family, of no distinction save the courage and cheerfulness that he saw all around him. And so it turned out. The Robinsons were five, though they later acquired some in-laws: John, the father, a soldier in the First World War and back in uniform in the Home Guard; his wife; two sons, Dick in the Auxiliary Fire Service and Andy in the RAF, training to be a pilot; and a daughter Kay, a munitions worker. Their home, 88 Ashleigh Road, was "an ordinary, common little semi-detached house, like thousands of other homes in England . . . bit of garden in front, bit of garden behind . . . three or four bedrooms upstairs . . . kitchen, parlour and dining room downstairs . . . front doorstep carefully scrubbed . . . . "

The show first went on the air to North America on April 4, 1941, while the Blitz was still in full force and the United States was still nine months away from entering the war. Two years later, in an anniversary programme, the narrator recalled that "every night, under Alan Melville's guidance, they told the world what it was like to live and work in a front line city. And day by day as their story unfolded it began to grip the attention of listeners all over the world. And nobody—not even Melville, and least of all the Robinsons—dreamed how fascinating that story was to become."

"Front Line Family" was to grip the attention of many listeners in Britain as well. The radio critics of some London newspapers heard the first episodes as they went over short wave, and liked them so much that they quickly demanded the programme for the British audience. So the BBC included it in its domestic schedule. But Bushnell had to follow the fortunes of the Robinsons from Canada. He had been recalled to his post as head of CBC programming two months before "Front Line Family" went on the air. He was followed at a few months' interval by Arthur Holmes. The bombing had died down, it was going to be a long while before any Canadian troops moved out of England, and it was time to go home and work on the assembly of equipment.

War production was getting into its stride, and Holmes found the vehicle he wanted in the Army's HUP, which stood for Heavy Utility Personnel carrier. It was of reasonable size, not a monster like the first van, and built to travel on roads full of other army vehicles; yet it was big enough to carry two turntables and all the other gear necessary to a mobile studio. And then work got started on the all-important portable units, units which could go in a jeep where the HUP could not go, or be carried by hand where a jeep could not go. They meant that no part of the battlefield would be inaccessible to our microphones.

3–DIEPPE

Bowman went home too, this time because of an invitation to make a cross-country speaking tour to workers in Canadian war industry plants. The visit kept him longer than he expected, for out of his tour grew a thirteen-week series of programmes on Canada's growing war production. It ran on the BBC's home and overseas services as well as on the CBC network. He could be away well enough. Thanks to recent additions, there were enough staff in London to look after programme commitments although these had increased. With the worst of the bombing past and no second front in the offing, attention was turned to other matters and other perils: German successes in Russia, and after Pearl Harbor, the far-ranging Japanese conquests in the Pacific; the swaying fortunes of the desert war in North Africa; and always, the Battle of the Atlantic.

With four crossings behind him, Bowman was already something of an authority on the Battle of the Atlantic. He was more so by the end of his fifth. He went back to London early in 1942, electing to sail with the navy again. It was March, one of the worst times for weather in the North Atlantic. Here is his account:

I sailed in the corvette *Midland*, escorting a convoy from Halifax to St. John's. At St. John's I transferred to a former American four-stacker, the *St. Francis*, and picked up another convoy. *Restigouche* was the senior ship, with my old friend Debbie Piers now in command. The convoy was 76 merchant ships and the speed four and half knots.

28

This when submarine warfare was at its height. I never thought we would get there safely. We lost the convoy in a bad storm and it took us three days to round up the ships, and 26 days to get to London-derry, but we were never attacked.

I'll never forget arriving at the Savoy Hotel after nearly a month travelling without a bath. My suitcase was soaking wet from salt water that had flooded the *St. Francis* during the storm. When I got to my room there was a phone in the bathroom and I phoned my friends as I soaked in the bath. When I went back into my bedroom the maids had taken all the stuff from my suitcase, and it came back next morning washed and ironed.

So he was back in plenty of time to go with the 2nd Canadian Division on the Dieppe Raid of August 19, 1942, the costly and tragic operation that has been argued about ever since but is considered by many military historians, as it was immediately after the event by the most responsible military authorities, to have been a necessary prelude to the eventual invasion of Europe. The plan was to capture Dieppe, demolish the port installations, gain knowledge of the state of the Germans' coastal defences, and withdraw when these objectives had been achieved. A combination of accidents, including the loss of surprise in one sector, turned the raid into a disaster.

Bowman was on both the abortive attempt of early July and the actual raid. The first attempt had to be called off because of weather, and the troops disembarked and returned to their camps after waiting on board their landing ships in the Solent for almost a week. Bob was to land with the Royal Hamilton Light Infantry, but until the time of sailing should arrive, he and all the other correspondents were kept together in a former ferry boat converted into an anti-aircraft ship. Many years afterwards he gave these reminiscences of the waiting period and subsequent events:

We got on board just before lunch, and somebody started a crap game which I got into although I am the worst gambler in the world. When the call for lunch came I found my pockets stuffed with bank notes, and I didn't like it a bit. My gambling luck had never been good, and if my luck was going to change I did not want it to change now. So I got rid of that money as fast as I could by not allowing anybody to buy a drink at the bar while we were on the ship.

Imagine my surprise when some weeks later I got the code message

"The balloon is up," and was asked to report to an address in Bath. Here I found the war correspondents assembled again, only this time they made us take off our correspondents' badges and put up the pips of second lieutenants instead. There never was a worse looking bunch of second lieutenants in any army, and as Bath was a training centre for the Coldstream Guards we certainly looked out of place. It must have been easy for any trained soldier to spot us as phoneys.

Fred Griffin of the Toronto *Star* was a recent arrival and hadn't got his uniform yet [Griffin had been over earlier, at the time of Dunkirk, and had covered the return of the BEF in magnificent despatches to his paper] so Cliff Wallace, who was a Canadian Army public relations officer with the rank of major, dressed Fred in his battledress. One Sunday morning Fred and I were out for a walk through the deserted streets of Bath when along came a battalion of Coldstream Guards on church parade. I told Fred: "Those men will give us a salute when they pass, and as you are a major and I'm only a second lieutenant, you'll have to acknowledge it." Fred was brave enough to go on the Dieppe raid, but he wasn't brave enough to take the salute. He immediately fled into the doorway of a chemist's shop and stood there with his back to the parade, leaving me to do the honours.

We were briefed for the raid by Cliff Wallace, who gathered the correspondents in a lattice-work summer house in the middle of a park, which nobody could approach without being seen, and he kept me on sentry duty outside while he put the others into the picture. I didn't know until they came out where we were going, and Cliff told me: "It's Dieppe."

When the real raid came, Bowman was on board a tank landing craft. This time he was to land with the Calgary Tank Regiment. The landing craft never got in to the beach, but instead lay for eight hours in Dieppe harbour, a target for bomb and shell fire, all its attempts to get in and land its tanks unsuccessful. His broadcast to Canada after he had got back across the Channel with the remnant of the 2nd Division was a selection from the notes he had scribbled as the flotilla approached the French coast and as his landing craft lay under fire.

And now I am just going to quote from the notes I took as we went along—some written in the darkness, and some written under heavy gun-fire so they are now smeared and dirty from the cordite. . . . On the way over I went to sleep for a while and then I went up on the open bridge with the young captain, a sub-lieutenant in the RNVR. And now from my notes just as they were written.

A-A tracers, like red sparks, and there is a heavy red glow extending down the coast. Our bombers are at work—more heavy flashes of coastal guns and bombs. Our aircraft are flying in close to the water and over us, and now dawn is breaking, also like a heavy barrage to the east. There are puffs of smoke in the sky, evidently from heavy German ack-ack batteries, and the ships are weaving in. Our lads are calm and the tank men, wearing black berets and sitting comfortably anywhere, are watching the action. The sky is becoming full of aircraft and the bombardment is becoming intense. Heavy thuds are shaking us even this far out to sea.

The captain is calmly steering us "Port 10 . . . midship." One bright fire is burning on the port horizon. Our medical men have put on their steel helmets and the guns are quieter. Perhaps the commandos have landed and are fixing them. The destroyers are holding their fire and are slinking along beside us. The ships are spread out behind us in long lines with gun crews mounted, each flying a black flag and a white ensign. There are fighter-patrols like flocks of geese high up and the bombers are scurrying home in the low haze over the water. The fighters look like swallows but in geese formation.

It is now 5:50 in the morning. Fast troop-carrying ships are starting to pass us now. And there is a French chasseur carrying French commandos. The coast has suddenly loomed up in front of us with its white hills and its cliffs, and it looks like a race to see who will get into action first. The sky is streaked with "flying fools" and so is the ocean. The destroyers are laying a smoke screen to windward and now they are turning broadside and are plastering the town with their guns. The smoke screen is lifting and I can see ships everywhere. The small troop-carrying landing craft are moving in lines under the artillery barrage. A Spitfire has just crashed off our starboard bow, and into the sea like a stone. We could see the pilot trying to get out but he couldn't.

The troops are heading for the beaches on either side of the town— the Royal Regiment to the left and the South Saskatchewan and the Queen's Own Camerons to the right. The Hamiltons and the Essex Scottish are going into the centre and we are following. Two Messerschmitts have just tried to attack us, and a ship behind us has just shot one of them into the sea.

Our tank troop captain has come up to the bridge to warn the captain, and it is only a few minutes until our zero time. He wants to get going, so we hoist our signal now, meaning we're shore-bound, and in we go.

It is now 6:45. Planes are everywhere overhead, and the shore guns are firing at us and at the small troop-carrying craft ahead of us. I can see casualties—men are in the water. Our tanks are warming up and they are starting to climb the ramp which will go down like a drawbridge when we reach the beach. Machine-gun bullets are whining around us, but our guns are cracking too at the aircraft over us. A tank landing craft is getting its tanks off behind the troops storming the beach, and heavy bombs have just dropped astern of us. It is a heavy Junkers and he is trying to stagger in to shore. He is full of lead from our guns. The tank landing craft ahead of us got her tanks ashore but she is sinking now and trying to get out, and we are being stopped by orders from going in, with destroyers laying a smoke screen around us.

There is heavy German gun-fire from a tobacco factory. I can see it sweeping the beach. Another Messerschmitt is down. The "ack-ack" fire is wonderful and a heavy bomber has just been driven off. He was trying to sneak in on our right; but a destroyer's guns got that one. Our tank men are disappointed, but now comes an order to try and come in again and they are delighted. The German shore batteries are still active. They are firing at us. Four Focke-Wulf bombers have just dived on us and two of them disappeared in flames. Our barrage is unbelievable and I am covered in black soot. Shells are falling on all sides of us, but we cannot get in to the beach, and we are ordered again to retire.

Three pilots are coming down by parachute. Another tank-landing craft has managed to get in but has been hit. Some casualties have just been brought out to our ship and the padre of the Fusiliers de Montréal told me about trying to get on shore. Men were killed all around him and one lieutenant had a bullet in his arm while he was trying to push the padre down.

It is now 9:25. The Germans on the cliffs are even throwing hand grenades on our ships below. Nine Heinkel bombers just passed overhead and I saw their bombs leave the aircraft; but I was too interested to watch the guns firing or where the bombs landed. They were aimed at the destroyers ahead of us, but they missed them. We were heavily attacked again and the convoy guns have just brought down two more Junkers. There was just a sort of flash of flame and the bombers came down like leaves in the wind. And now dive bombers are attacking us. One of them has just been shot into the sea.

Strong reinforcements of our fighters are arriving and they are flying low around us to protect us from the dive-bombers. We can't get in to the beach. We have tried again but bombs and gun-fire are driving us out. I have just been knocked down by a heavy bomb, in fact a stick of four bombs; a very near miss to starboard. Some of our men are wounded. One of them is dead. Our fighters are wonderful, and they are fearless and they are trying to protect our men on the beaches who are being re-embarked.

Our aircraft are suffering heavily, and I have seen several of them come down in flames over Dieppe. The wounded are being brought off, but we hear that we have landed on every beach. Evidently the engineers have suffered heavily, and were unable to blast a way for the tanks for about an hour. The tanks formed a square on the field and they are protecting our men while being re-embarked. The colonel of our tanks has attacked a machine-gun post on foot. The South Saskatchewans got in safely but the Queen's Own Camerons following them have been hit by six-inch howitzers, and there are casualties.

I am listening to our tank short wave equipment and I know they are fighting like fools on shore. I can hear one of our tank captains saying "Come on over, boys, we are killing lots of Germans." We are ordered to manoeuvre out of the harbour. It is afternoon now, but the destroyers are remaining behind just a few hundred yards off the shore, and they are sending in small boats to get our men who can get away. They are wonderful. We have been here eight hours now, and small craft are streaming out under bombs and gun-fire.

Bowman kept those notes as a souvenir. He also kept a photograph which Fred Griffin gave him afterwards. Griffin, in another tank landing craft, with Lieutenant Frank Royal of the Army Film and Photo Unit, a few hundred yards to port, watched one of the attacks on Bob's ship by a group of dive bombers, saw the bombs fall, and said, "There goes Bowman." Royal snapped his shutter at the instant that spouts of water hid the landing craft as the bombs straddled it

When the correspondents got back to London there was a briefing set up for them. They were told that in the air at least, Dieppe had been a victory, and that the Germans had lost three planes for every one of ours shot down. That story was demolished by Group Captain J. E. Johnson in his book *Wing Leader*. Johnson wrote that our fighter cover had been all but overwhelmed and that our air losses far outnumbered the enemy's. He told how he escaped from two German fighters by diving low over our ships and taking the chance of being shot down by their anti-aircraft fire. Bob thought that must have been the narrow escape he saw. "I remember," he recalled, "seeing a

Spitfire race practically through our masts. Of course our guns were blazing at him too."

In spite of the raid's bitter outcome, Bowman kept his respect for the way it was marshalled. He said, in the 1960 broadcast in which he recalled the aborted raid in July and the rendezvous at Bath:

I am speaking from memory now, but about 1,000 ships had to assemble in the middle of the Channel in the dark of night and get into formation. In order to make this rendezvous in time they had to leave many parts of Britain at carefully calculated times, and achieve perfect navigation to get to their longitude spot on the dot of a nighttime hour.

There were only two or three little ships with us when we sailed from Newhaven. When dawn came there were a thousand ships in perfect formation. They had arrived on time, got into formation in the dark, and then been swept safely through the German minefields. What a demonstration!

Dieppe was Bowman's first and last battle. It was ironical that he was not to be with the Overseas Unit that he had started when the really big balloon went up. He was called home on another of his special missions, this time conducting a party of soldiers who had fought at Dieppe. It was his job to introduce them at patriotic rallies. Then, before he could get back to London, there came a request from the British Ministry of Information for him to go with Leonard W. Brockington on a four-month speaking tour in Australia and New Zealand. These countries were naturally preoccupied with the war in the Pacific and the fact that the United States was their protector. The ministry thought it was a good idea for Brockington to go and remind them of the British struggle against Germany. Since Brockington's health was uncertain, they wanted Bowman to go with him in case a substitute speaker became necessary.

He came back from the Pacific thinking he would soon be in London again. He had left all his possessions there, expecting to be back long before. But he found things different in the CBC. For one thing, a new general manager had replaced his old friend Gladstone Murray. He found himself at odds with management. The expected permission to go back to London never

came. When he put in his resignation, it was accepted. Where-
ever the blame for the parting lay, the corporation owed him
much at his going.

4–WAITING

The thought of a second front could never be quieted for long, and as 1942 lengthened, public expectation was growing that 1943 would be the year for it. The CBC, which had invoked high powers to get its men into France in 1940, began to get ready again. Now there was a whole Canadian Army instead of a single division, and there was a huge air force. It would have to be an enlarged effort.

Bowman was gone. Holmes would return in time for the fighting. Bert Altherr, who had been rushed across the Atlantic to be the engineer on the expected move to France, had been kept in Canada after his voyage with Bowman in *Restigouche* in 1941. Gerard Arthur had gone back, as had Jacques Desbaillets, who had succeeded him. Harold Wadsworth, an engineer from Ottawa, had been over and gone back, but would return. There were in London H. Rooney Pelletier from Montreal, who had taken Bowman's place; Gerry Wilmot, in charge of troop entertainment, and his assistant Jack Peach, who had come to the unit from Vancouver at the height of the Blitz but was shortly to transfer to RCAF Public Relations; and two engineers, Paul Johnson and Alec MacDonald.

Pelletier had been offered a job with the BBC and wanted to go, so the first thing was to replace him. His replacement was John Kannawin, who had been in charge of CBC's Prairie Region. He went over in mid-November of 1942. He was followed in approximately this order by Peter Stursberg, Paul Dupuis,

36

Andrew Cowan, the returning Arthur Holmes, A. E. Powley, Lloyd Moore, Matthew Halton, Marcel Ouimet, Paul Barette and Benoit Lafleur, Joseph Beauregard, Wadsworth, Bill Herbert, Clifford Speer, Fred McCord and Laurence Marshall. Wadsworth, Moore, Beauregard, Speer, McCord and Marshall were engineers. Moore had no long journey to join the unit, since he was already in England as an officer in the Tank Corps when the CBC obtained his release and transfer. All were to get through safely except Cliff Speer, who died shortly after V-E Day as the result of a traffic accident in London.

Kannawin, the first of the new wave, went over in November, 1942, by air, thus becoming a pioneer of transatlantic flying. Today's inter-continental aviation is a child of the Second World War, and in 1942 it was a very young child. Having first signed a form releasing everybody from liability for anything that might happen to him, Kannawin went on board a Liberator bomber. He flew lying on a mattress on the bomber's floor and wearing flying suit, flying boots, helmet, mitts, oxygen mask, parachute pack and life jacket. "Ye Gods," he had confided to his diary before take-off, "What would I do even if I did manage to pull the rip cord?" It was a long flight: four hours from Dorval to Gander and another eleven to an airport near Prestwick in Scotland.

He was followed by Peter Stursberg, travelling more conventionally in a freighter full of high explosive. Stursberg had been an editor in the Vancouver newsroom, with considerable experience in special events broadcasting. Hard after him came Paul Dupuis from the announcing staff at Montreal and Andrew Cowan from the Talks Department in Toronto. Dupuis was to achieve stardom in British films after the war. For Cowan it was the beginning of an eleven-year assignment overseas. After a brief spell in Canada at the end of the war, he went back to take charge of the London office at the beginning of 1946 and stayed till 1954, when he came home to be the director of the CBC's Northern and Armed Forces Services.

Matthew Halton was already a famous journalist and broadcaster. As European correspondent of the Toronto *Star* he had been writing about the Nazi menace for years before the war, when it was a most unpopular thing to do. He had been in London during the Battle of Britain and the Blitz. His last assignment for his paper had been to spend almost two years in North Africa with the Eighth Army. When invited to become the CBC's senior war correspondent he delayed only to finish his book on the desert war, *Ten Years to Alamein*.

Marcel Ouimet had been head of the combined French-English newsroom in Montreal, and Barette and Lafleur were members of his staff. They came principally to serve the French language audience, but Ouimet doubled in English.

The last of the broadcasters to join the unit was Bill Herbert, a cheerful and energetic young announcer and former newspaperman from the Vancouver studios. He had enlisted and was in the army when the CBC got him released to be a war correspondent. Bill got to London towards the end of April, 1944—in time to go to Normandy with the first RCAF fighter squadrons that followed the D Day landings. He changed from Air Force blue into khaki when he went from France to Italy to cover the Canadians' last months of fighting there. When he went home to Vancouver after the end of the war in Europe, it was in the hope of getting to the war in the Far East. The Japanese surrender put an end to that idea, and apparently to his days as a war correspondent, but he was to get into battle again within a few years, covering the Korean War. In the meantime and subsequently, he pursued his broadcasting career at home with customary vigour and distinction, and for many years was as well-known throughout Canada for his part in the CBC's major special events programmes as he had formerly been for his war reports. After his return from the war in Europe he had changed his uniform yet again, this time to become an officer in the Royal Canadian Navy (Reserve), in which he rose to the rank of captain before the onset of the long illness from which he died in 1974.

The roll call must also include Don Fairbairn, an excellent and indefatigable broadcaster, who probably put as many reports on the air as anybody and whom we all considered one of us, although he belonged to the air force. He had been a CBC farm commentator before joining the RCAF. While the rest of us enjoyed the privileges and facilities afforded to war correspondents, he did most of his war reporting, until he was commissioned at the end of 1944, while serving in the rank of corporal. He managed to be an extraordinary NCO.

And here too mention must be made of Eddie Baudry, who wasn't a member of the unit either, but who was the only man to lose his life while serving it in a war theatre.

One of the first jobs that devolved on John Kannawin after he reached London at the end of 1942 was to see Eddie Baudry off to Algiers, where he was to be the CBC's temporary correspondent at Allied Forces Headquarters. Baudry, a Belgian national, had been working in Montreal when the war broke out. Hastening home, he served in the Belgian Army until the capitulation, then joined the staff of the exiled Belgian government in London. There he met Rooney Pelletier, Kannawin's predecessor, who arranged for his secondment. It was December 3 when Kannawin saw him off. A little less than two months later he got a call from the Belgian government to say that it wanted him back immediately. He sent a cable, but communication with the Mediterranean was slow and the cable didn't get there in time. Instead of a reply, he got word that Eddie Baudry was dead, shot while flying to cover the conference between Churchill, Roosevelt and the Joint Chiefs of Staff at Casablanca in French Morocco. It was at the Casablanca Conference, incidentally, that the decision was made to invade Sicily in the coming summer and Western Europe in 1944. It was from Alan Moorehead, then a famous British war correspondent and later famous as an author, that Kannawin learned the details. This from his diary:

Alan Moorehead called me. . . . I had been expecting to hear from him about Baudry. They were together on the flight to Casablanca. Laurie Audrain got us together for lunch. Had a long and sad conversation about Eddie. I shall write it down while it is fresh in my mind.

The morning of the day Baudry was killed fifteen correspondents and crew took off for Casablanca in a DC3. They had what proved to be an inexperienced young American pilot in charge. They left very early in the morning and when about an hour out the wings started to ice up badly. The pilot elected to take the sea route and came down very low over the Med. They passed Gib. and then turned south. Eventually they arrived over the beach of Spanish Morocco and the inexperienced pilot stooged around trying to get his bearings. Ack-ack opened up on them but he didn't seem to realize it. Finally he came to a town which was obviously Spanish to the correspondents. Moorehead had a map and could read Spanish names below him. But the pilot thought he was over French territory and circled the town for the better part of an hour, radioing down and simply receiving jumbled Morse in reply. Then machine-gun fire came up and a bullet through the cockpit grazed the head of the co-pilot. A second burst came through the fuselage and everyone ducked to the floor except Baudry, who simply fell back with a gaping wound in his head. Moorehead was sitting beside him and he lowered him to the floor, where they rested his head on a parachute pack. But Baudry was bleeding horribly and obviously dying. They bandaged him as best they could. The pilot finally got on his course, radioed ahead, and when the aircraft landed at Casablanca an ambulance was there to rush Baudry to hospital. He died en route. The following morning the incident came to the personal attention of President Roosevelt, who sent up a wreath and ordered an American military funeral for Baudry. Official PR photos were taken and Moorehead was kind enough to give me two sets. I sent one of them on immediately to Baudry's widow. So finally the story of Eddie's ill-fated assignment is concluded.

The month of this entry in Kannawin's diary, March, 1943, saw a great stir in army circles and in the English countryside. It was exercise SPARTAN, the rehearsal for an invasion of Europe in which General McNaughton, commanding a "British" army (it was actually his own First Canadian Army), had the task of breaking out of a bridgehead and defeating the defending "German" army (actually British).

General McNaughton had long been the choice of the planners for a leading role, if not *the* leading role, in the invasion when it came. He was to command the initial assault, to be made by troops of the British Army, and then, the landing made, to lead the breakout and exploitation with his own Canadian Army. It was a glittering prospect. Peter Stursberg, who covered the exercise and sent home nightly reports, had no way of knowing that SPARTAN was to be a test of McNaughton as a commander in the field, that critical eyes in the higher command were on him, and that the difficulties he experienced were to weigh against him.

McNaughton made his breakout and defeated the "enemy" force, but there were awkward moments on the way. The Canadian official historian has attributed these to McNaughton's insistence on employing, alongside his admirably trained and efficient 1st Corps, the newly-formed, largely untrained and completely unshaken down 2nd Canadian Corps instead of the experienced British corps he was offered—on the ground that the primary purpose of an exercise was the training of troops. History might have been different if he had taken the British corps and been able to conduct the exercise with flawless efficiency.

But these mighty matters were all a closed book to Peter and his fellow correspondents, who found the whole thing rather a lark as they drove from point to point in cars or jeeps provided by a thoughtful army, enjoying the spectacle of monumental traffic jams in narrow village streets or of farmers holding fists to heaven as tanks tore paths of ruin through their crops.

I got to London in early May with the returning Arthur Holmes, who had been my companion across the Atlantic on the freighter *Gdynia*. At 2600 hundred tons gross she must have been one of the smallest ships in the convoy trade, and the scars from a battle with U-boats on her westbound passage were an immediate encouragement as we climbed aboard her in Bedford Basin. Her cargo was heavy machinery, and when a passenger asked if we ought to sleep with our clothes on, her Swedish captain shook his head. "Thees sheep," he said, "wouldn't last two minutes."

My sailing was due to the CBC's realization that the looming job of war reporting was going to be too big for remote control and would require someone in charge on the spot. It was going to be the responsibility of D. C. McArthur, head of the CBC News Service, and as the senior member of McArthur's staff I got the job. The catch in it was that while the others were headed for the battlefield, my duty would be to sit in London, make godlike decisions—most of them obvious enough, thank heaven—as to who should go where, keep in touch with our men after they had got to the front, and maintain an unremitting vigilance to see that their reports got home. Things turned out a bit better than that, and opportunities came for me to get away and see a bit of the war for myself.

Arthur Holmes was annoyed when we landed. It had been a normal enough crossing for the time: fog off Newfoundland; three days of steaming alone between losing the convoy and catching up again; after that, a lot of depth charging and the news one day that the escort had destroyed a submarine. But some of our stragglers were lost. When we got to Liverpool the captain, after he had seen the naval authorities, told us that six ships had been sunk. After we got to London one of our fellow passengers, who worked in the Ministry of Shipping, told Holmes—whether accurately or not we didn't find out—that the number had risen to fourteen.

While we waited around at Halifax, Arthur had learned that the *Queen Elizabeth* was to sail from New York in a few days, and that we could get space in her. He had had plenty of experience with convoys, and the thought of a safe and speedy dash across in one of the Queens was appealing, so he telephoned the CBC official who looked after the shipment of war correspondents and asked him to switch our bookings. He was turned down. Now Arthur felt the urge to plant remorse in the adamant official's heart. The problem was how to do it. Anything he wrote was sure to be censored before it got out of England. He solved it with a long and rambling letter which contained a brief paragraph, practically a parenthesis: "You know that ball game we were going to just before we left. It was a good game but we lost, fourteen to one."

Whether struck by remorse or not, the recipient kept the letter and showed it to Holmes after the war. All sorts of innocent things had been scissored out, but the tally of losses had got through.

Spring, 1943 was an interesting time to get to London. For one thing, the Germans were stepping up their air raids. One started almost as soon as we got off the train, and the performance was repeated on each of the next four nights. That was something to be expected. There was more to be concerned about in the feeling that something important was going to happen soon, and the anxiety as to whether the unit would be at strength in time for it. Halton was coming, but he had to finish off his book first. When I had said goodbye to Ouimet and his colleagues in Montreal on the way to Halifax it was still not settled when they would leave. In the event, the troops who were to invade Sicily were already on board ship and waiting to sail when Halton, Ouimet, Barette and Lafleur got across, but it didn't matter. There were only two places for war correspondents with the Canadians in the Sicilian landing, one for the CBC and one for The Canadian Press, and Peter Stursberg had gone for us.

The call, when it came, was sudden as well as secret. In addition to Stursberg himself, only John Kannawin and I were permitted to know of it. Peter was called down to Canadian Military Headquarters on the morning of June 11 and told that he was to leave London that night for a destination that he would learn in due time. CMHQ were quite glad when he told them he had an appointment to interview H. G. Wells that afternoon for a programme that would be heard in Canada about two weeks later. They told him to go ahead, since the delayed broadcast would make a good cover for his movement. So he did the interview and in the evening stole away at the appointed hour to the appointed railway station, where he met Ross Munro of The Canadian Press and with him caught a train to Scotland.

The engineers Paul Johnson and Alec MacDonald followed on June 20, with the first of the new Holmes-designed recording vans. The portable unit, for use in places where the van couldn't go, went forward in the care of the Army to a destination that was secret. Johnson was under the instruction to pick it up, when it became fitting to know where it was, and take it to wherever Stursberg might be. Andrew Cowan's departure on the 21st was less mysterious. He was bound for Allied Forces Headquarters for the Mediterranean, and everybody knew that was at Algiers. Matthew Halton flew in from Canada on June 20, and Ouimet, Barette and Lafleur, who had come by ship, arrived the next day. Stursberg had by then been more than a week with the Canadian First Division in the River Clyde.

5–SICILY

In the Clyde, Stursberg saw something of the gathering of what was to be the greatest armada yet seen. When this fleet made its rendezvous in the Mediterranean with ships from other ports in Britain, from the United States and from North Africa, the assembly would number more than 3,000 ships in all—merchant ships, warships and landing craft large and small. He and Munro were together in a ship carrying 3,500 men of the 1st Division, including the Royal Canadian Regiment, one of the assault battalions in whatever was coming up. The ship was part of the Fast Assault Convoy, under the command of Admiral Philip Vian, "Vian of the *Cossack*," hero of a resounding naval exploit in the early days of the war. The Fast Assault Convoy was to sail last, and overtake at the rendezvous the slower convoys that had preceded it.

Just before it sailed on June 28, Stursberg and Munro were summoned to a briefing by Major General Guy Simonds, the divisional commander, on board the headquarters ship, HMS *Hilary*. They were told that the division was on its way to the Mediterranean, where it would join the Eighth Army in an important combined operation. A little more came next day when the convoy was at sea and Admiral Vian signalled all hands: "We are on our way to the Mediterranean to take part in the greatest combined operation ever attempted." The troops were told on July 1, Dominion Day, that the target was Sicily and the 1st Division was to land at the Pachino peninsula, the southern tip of the island.

44

The storm that blew up in the Mediterranean on July 9, the day before the invasion was to start, threatened the whole combined operation for a time, and delayed the CBC's first landing. It died down in the evening, but left a heavy swell which made it very difficult for the landing craft to manoeuvre alongside the ships and embark their troops. Landings which were to have been made closer to midnight than dawn were held up for hours.

The two tank landing craft that were to take in the assault companies of the RCR had an especially hard time, and daylight was beginning when they got away from the ship. So it was full day when Stursberg got into a landing craft with some of the follow-up troops, wearing one life jacket and carrying his typewriter wrapped in another. On the run in, the men heard a BBC news broadcast announcing the invasion. It was based of course on the pre-arranged communiques. Peter noted one soldier who stared hard at the radio and said: "Now how did they get the news so quickly?"

The Canadians in the assault had to trans-ship again close in to shore, into amphibious vehicles called DUKW's, because there were sandbars in front of their beaches. The "duck" that carried Peter landed him dry shod. Under the naval gunfire that covered the landings, the few Italian troops manning the defences had retreated inland, there to surrender at the first opportunity, and not a shot had been fired at the RCR's assault companies. They had gone forward to capture the Pachino airfield, their first objective. Ross Munro had landed somewhere else with their conducting officer, Captain Dave McLellan. The troops Stursberg had landed with had gone forward to their task. He was on his own. So he sat down on a sand dune, unwrapped his typewriter from its life preserver, and started to write his first report from the war.

It took some days of walking in pursuit of a fast-moving front before he caught up with Munro and McLellan. They had just got hold of a jeep, so Peter attached himself along with two officers of the Film and Photo Unit who happened along. The overloading they thus imposed caused them to christen the jeep "The Poor Little Thing." They had barely started when they saw, coming from the opposite direction, the unlikely sight of a large civilian car with an Italian soldier at the wheel and a mixed cargo of one Canadian officer, one civilian and three Italian officers. When the car turned in to an olive grove they followed it, thus to become spectators at the surrender of the first Italian general taken prisoner in the campaign.

The Canadians had been on the point of attacking the town of Modica, where the Italian division supposed to be defending the coastal area had its headquarters, when a civilian messenger came out with the word that the garrison commander wished to spare the town by surrendering. The brigade major of the 2nd Brigade, Major R. S. Malone, decided to test the story, so he drove into the town in a jeep, flying a white handkerchief for a flag of truce, while a couple of armoured cars stood by in case of trouble. The garrison commander, a Major General Achille D'Avet, confirmed his wish to surrender but insisted that he should do so only to an officer of equal rank. Malone was obliging and offered to take him to Major General Simonds. The general also insisted that he should surrender his pistol, in token of his sword, to no-one but General Simonds, and again Malone was obliging; having demanded the pistol and taken out the cartridges, he handed it back to the general and let him keep it for the ceremony. The matter of transport became a problem when the general wanted to be accompanied by three of his staff and the mayor of the town. That was too much of a crowd for an army jeep, so they all got somehow into the general's car. Since Malone had taken the precaution of leaving his own driver as guard on the general's operations room, the general's driver had to be pressed into service.

The formalities were completed to everybody's satisfaction at General Simonds' headquarters, and since General D'Avet would be having no further use for his car, Major Malone appropriated it. He had a moment's apprehension, though, as he was inspecting his trophy after the ceremony, when General Simonds himself walked up and cast an appraising eye over it. The handkerchief that did duty as a flag of truce reposes to this day as a memento in a Sussex manor house whose owner had been a friend to the 1st Division during its years in England.

Dick Malone was to be paterfamilias to the correspondents with the Canadians on both the Italian and Western fronts. After serving for some months on General Montgomery's staff as senior liaison officer, he took charge of Canadian Army Public Relations in Italy for a few months before returning to England to take command of No. 3 P.R. Group. That meant being in charge of all the multitudinous arrangements which enabled the correspondents to follow 1st Canadian Army from D Day on. He ended his war on the deck of USS *Missouri*, in Tokyo Bay, at the Japanese surrender, and soon afterwards published a book of wartime reminiscences under the title *Missing From The Record*. He later became president of FP Publications and publisher of the Toronto *Globe and Mail*.

It was annoying that at first Stursberg could only cable his reports, since the landing arrangements could make no room for an engineer and equipment. He was glad enough to get a signal telling him to get to Algiers at the first pause in the fighting, use the transmitter there for the broadcasts he had been saving up, and then try and get Johnson and the portable to Sicily with him. He saw his opportunity when the Canadians had captured Leonforte. Getting to Algiers was no problem, and neither were the broadcasts. With nearly two weeks of campaigning to talk about, he reeled off half a dozen of them. The problems were first, how to get back to Sicily himself—all the planes seemed to be full of people with a higher priority than a war correspondent's—and second, how to get Paul and the portable away without causing a storm of protest to the army public relations people from all the distinguished Canadian journalists who were kicking their heels in frustration in North Africa.

Just about every Canadian correspondent in London had wanted to go to Sicily. But Supreme Headquarters controlled the admissions. Canadian Army Public Relations had taken a chance and shipped a number of correspondents to North Africa in the hope that seeing them there, the higher authorities would relent and let them into Sicily. But the higher authorities took their time about relenting, so there were a lot of frustrated people in Algiers and Tunis. Stursberg and Johnson learned that the chances of getting air space to Sicily were better in Tunis than in Algiers, so to Tunis they went, and there they found that by some miracle they could fly the next morning. Very early and very silently, lest they should awaken and enrage any of their stranded colleagues, they stole out of their hotel carrying the portable unit between them. They were at the front, after some hitch-hiking, that evening. A couple of days later a friend in the BBC, who had been listening to an incoming transmission, walked up to my desk and said: "Congratulations. You've got the first sound out of conquered territory."

The Canadians had just captured the mountain town of Agira when Stursberg and Johnson reached the front, and the next evening the pipes and drums of the Seaforth Highlanders of Canada played "Retreat" in the town square "to the huge delight of the assembled townspeople" as Colonel G. W. L. Nicholson says in his official history *The Canadians in Italy*. It was a wonderful opportunity to put the portable to its first use. The pipes and drums, echoing across the square, made a grand recording, and with Stursberg's commentary before and after the music, the whole ceremony made a good broadcast. The Seaforths had their own gratification out of it too, for they heard it next evening over the BBC. In exchange for the use of their receiving and transmitting facilities—they provided the pick-up point for our incoming signals, and our programmes crossed the Atlantic in their North American service—the BBC were entitled to the use of any of our programmes in any of their services except those heard in Canada.

The broadcast of the Seaforths' pipes and drums followed what was to be the route for all our reports from Sicily and Italy: the recording was flown to Algiers, put on the air there on a beam directed at London, re-recorded in London for transmission across the Atlantic, picked up and recorded at three points in Canada—Dartmouth, N.S., Britannia Heights just outside Ottawa, and Hornby, near Toronto—and fed over a land line, from whichever of the three points had the best reception, to the studio in Toronto or Montreal, which made the final recording, the one the audience would hear. All very old-fashioned now, and there was bound to be a slight loss of quality with each of the re-recordings, but it was the best that anyone could do then, and it worked. And old-fashioned or not, radio was instantaneous even then. A recording was no sooner on the transmitter than it was being heard in London, and so on, with allowance for the intervals between reception and transmission, all along the route to the studio.

The Algiers beam put a first class signal into London, and the transmissions across the Atlantic generally got through well. Sometimes it was perfect. Sometimes static interfered and the result was more or less distortion. On really bad days when the sun spots were acting up we would get a cable in London saying "Westdown," which meant that nothing intelligible was getting through. When that happened we simply repeated the transmission next day and hoped for better luck.

Stursberg and Johnson worked the portable unit hard up to the crossing of the Simeto River and the capture of Adrano. That was the end of the campaign as far as the Canadians were concerned, though the end did not come until some days later with the capture of Messina. Stursberg was under instructions to get to a live microphone—which meant Algiers—as fast as he could when the Canadians' part was over. The last use he made of the portable was to record a review of the Canadians' work by their commander, General Simonds. "What I want to emphasize," the general said, "is that all these operations have been successful because each arm and service has gone full out to do its share; and though the spectacular actions sometimes fall to individual units, and the infantry carry the brunt of the fighting, the ultimate success has resulted because of the contributions made by all." Then, leaving the portable in the charge of Johnson, to be taken over by Halton and Ouimet, Stursberg was off to Algiers.

It wasn't official that we were going to invade the mainland of Italy, but that was clearly going to happen, and Halton and Ouimet were in Sicily to be ready for it. Army public relations had kept in mind the Canadian need for reporting in both languages, and there were places in the initial landings for both of them. Johnson was to go with the portable unit, and MacDonald was to follow with the van. The 1st Canadian Division was to be one of the two assaulting divisions. The route was obviously across the Strait of Messina. The only thing uncertain was when.

Benoit Lafleur had somehow managed to land on Sicily with Ouimet, but was quickly bustled off the island and back to join the throng of restive correspondents in Algiers. What was more, the military people there took the view that he had no right in the theatre at all, since priorities were tight and there were already five CBC men there. They were going to send him back to London. On the very brink of this ignominy he wangled an accreditation to a force of French Moroccans that was going off to fight in Corsica. The Moroccans were Giraudists, not General de Gaulle's Free French, whom Benny preferred, but the point was too nice to count in a crisis. Off to Corsica he went in a French cruiser, and he had a couple of weeks there before the capture of the island was complete. There was a drawback in that there was no way of getting reports from Corsica back to Algiers and thence to Canada, but that was offset by the fact that he was the only Canadian correspondent there. When he got back to Algiers he spun out his exclusive reports on Corsica for the French network until even his gifts of description were exhausted and he had to fall back on local colour. But he kept his precious French accreditation, and so managed to be still in North Africa when it came time for him to go to Italy, fully accredited to the Canadians, to take Ouimet's place.

Stursberg heard the news of the capture of Messina and the end of the Sicilian campaign in Algiers. According to his records, he was instructed soon afterwards to get back to Sicily. He was nothing loath, since that would put him a step nearer Italy for the time when the admission of correspondents became freer. But getting to Sicily was a different matter from being told to, now that the fighting was over and people on official business were jamming every plane. Ernest Buritt of The Canadian Press was in the same fix, and the two of them were beginning to wonder if they'd ever get out of North Africa when Rod Mac-Innes told them how. MacInnes, later to become a vice-president of Air Canada, was a wing commander and chief public relations officer for the RCAF in the Mediterranean theatre. He told them that if they could get to Tunis, they could get on a plane. He not only told them, he drove them himself, a day and a half's journey. At Tunis two places opened up on the only plane leaving for Sicily that day. A succession of lifts took them up the crowded coast road to Catania and the headquarters of the 1st Division. They were met by Bill Gilchrist, the major in charge of public relations in that theatre.

"My God," said Gilchrist, "you certainly time things right. We're invading Italy tonight. Jump into the jeep and we'll go and see the fireworks."

The Sicily Landing, with Peter Stursberg in foreground

In Sicily, (left to right) Lt. Al Fraser, Ross Munro, Capt. Dave McLellan and Peter Stursberg

Sicily, (left to right) Matthew Halton, Capt. John Howard (conducting officer), Marcel Ouimet, Alec MacDonald, Paul Johnson and Peter Stursberg

Surrender in Sicily, (left to right) Maj. R. S. Malone, Maj.-Gen. Achille D'Avet, D'Avet's naval attache, Maj.-Gen. Guy Simonds

The Ortona Front, with (left to right) Holmes, Moore, Halton

Italy. Benoit Lafleur (with microphone) interviewing troops, with Joseph Beauregard in jeep

Gregory Clark (left) with Fred Griffin in Italy

Beauregard with portable and Italian children

Near Ortona, Moore (left) and Halton under a reminder of Southern Ontario

Marcel Ouimet on
the Adriatic Front

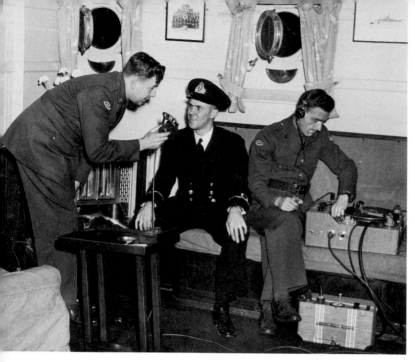

On board HMCS Restigouche, Bowman (left) and Altherr record an interview

Juno Beach, D Day

In Normandy Beachhead, the press camp shelled

Canadian patrol in Caen

The ruins of Falaise

Return to Dieppe: 2nd Canadian Division, 3 September 1944

They drove to a villa at Mili Marina, one of the embarkation beaches. Halton and Ouimet were already out in the Strait in their landing craft. Stursberg fell asleep. He was awakened by the eruption of the biggest barrage he had ever heard. He dashed to the roof. Later he wrote in his book, *Journey Into Victory*:

The flashes of the guns fused into one great flame which silhouetted the hills and seemed to lick around their sharp, crenellated edges as if it was devouring them. Above this fearful white inferno rose half a dozen searchlight beams, forming a majestic blue column against the backcloth of the sky. The searchlights were markers on which the landing craft would take their bearings.

6–SOUTHERN ITALY

In the 1960 radio programme in which Bowman and Holmes recounted their crossing with the 1st Division in 1939, Marcel Ouimet recalled the start of the Italian campaign in 1943:

By August 23, all along the coast of the Strait of Messina, material, ammunition and supplies were being accumulated at an amazing rate, this despite the difficult roads on which heavy trucks, jeeps, tanks, Bren gun carriers, the amphibious DUKW, medium and light guns— in other words all of the weapons of war which had followed the victor of Alamein through the campaign of Africa—were taking up position in what looked to me, a lay observer, like organized confusion.

In the Strait, units of the Royal Navy could be seen hourly: battleships, cruisers, destroyers. In the air, allied aircraft flying from the Sicilian airdromes or the airdromes of North Africa pounded roads, railroads, bridges and other military objectives in order to paralyze the moribund Italian war machine.

A few days before the crossing of the Strait and the assault on Reggio Calabria it was evident that the Italians had little fight left in them. Officers and soldiers of the coastal garrisons daily crossed the Strait in all kinds of craft to surrender. The partners of Hitler had lost their will to resist. We knew of three forts on the high ground near Reggio, but little resistance was expected. We knew the Germans were already pulling out, and on the night of September 2nd, before boarding the landing ships, we all slept quite soundly in our jeeps, parked in an olive grove near the small village of Santa Teresa.

The landing craft left the Sicilian coast during the night in dead silence. By two o'clock, they were receiving the protection of an artillery barrage. Seven hundred guns showered the opposite shore for two hours, while two thousand planes were ready to support the landing. It was a strange spectacle—all these guns vomiting fire and steel without a reply. It was more like fireworks than the prelude to a new and important military campaign.

As we boarded the ship, initial messages indicated that everything was going forward according to plan. A few hours later, the three forts and the Reggio airdrome were in our hands. One of the forts had fallen to the Royal 22nd Regiment, who had found the officers having breakfast in their well-pressed uniforms and freshly-polished boots while a few yards away navy guns lay idle, their caissons filled with shells.

This was the beginning of the Italian campaign. It was an easy start for the Canadians. A few days later, the Americans were to meet more stubborn opposition from the Germans at Salerno. By September 7th, the Italians were laying down their arms en masse. Of course, when we landed, we had no way of knowing that negotations for the surrender of the Italian army were already taking place.

Ross Munro said afterwards—at least I so quoted him in an article published in *Saturday Night* as a double-page spread under the heading "War Reporting Complete With Sound Effects Is Unique Contribution of CBC Overseas Unit"—that the most remarkable sight he saw on a night and morning of remarkable sights was that of Matt Halton and Paul Johnson wading ashore, each tenderly carrying aloft one of the two waterproofed cases that contained the portable unit.

They deposited the cases at the water's edge while Johnson looked for a sheltered place to put them. He saw it in a culvert a hundred yards or so down the beach. He shoved one of the cases under it and was halfway there with the second one when a Stuka bomber, the one enemy plane he saw, dived and dropped a bomb, the only bomb he heard explode that morning, precisely where the precious equipment had just been resting. Then he, Halton and the gear were off inland with the newly-landed brigade.

That was to cause Ouimet a lot of trouble and some rage. Marcel had made the crossing to Reggio in a less mellow mood than his subsequent broadcast would suggest. I got a letter from him when he had been in Italy a few weeks:

Matt Halton and Ross Munro were in one jeep. They had been stationed to the 3rd Brigade for the landing. You may know that this particular brigade is formed of the West Novas, the Carleton and York (half French) and the Royal 22nd (totally French). I had to land with the 2nd Brigade, the brigade of the westerners. On the first day I was cut off from the boys whose exploits I wanted to narrate. As it happened, fortunately enough, there were no exploits to be narrated.

The difficulty was that the army's system of priorities had put Halton with the assault brigade and Ouimet with the follow-up troops. It was compounded by the fact that Halton had Paul Johnson and the one portable unit with him, and then further compounded by the fact that the assault brigade, meeting no opposition, got inland farther and faster than was expected, so the pre-arranged rendezvous fell through. It took Ouimet two days of increasingly incensed searching before he caught up with Halton, and still they had only the one recording unit between them. The van was on the way, but it was caught somewhere in the traffic jam between Sicily and the front. And there was more than a traffic jam to contend with. Army PR had made splendid arrangements for the correspondents, including plenty of jeeps. "What's happened to them God only knows," Marcel's letter said. "Some say they were sunk on the way down."

Sunk they had been. The torpedoing of the *City of Venice*, the *St. Essylt* and the *Devis*, between Oran and Algiers while on their way to Sicily, had cost the 1st Canadian Division more than five hundred vehicles, and it was a long while before the shortage could be repaired. Our men were lucky to get the loan of one jeep, but even that was qualified luck. Ouimet's letter went on:

A few days later we agreed that the CBC party should travel together. So we all got in a jeep: the driver, the conducting officer, Matt, Johnson and I. And all our baggage. Necessarily, space could not be found for the equipment as well. PRO had no other jeep to give us, so we had to leave our recording apparatus behind, and we were without it for the duration of our push, except for a brief period when it caught up with us at Catanzaro. Last Sunday during the battle of Potenza, had we had our equipment we would have been able to make quite a recording. Unfortunately it was still on the way up.

Even the despatch rider system was poor. One DR was sent with us to carry the copy of all correspondents—there were seven of us since Ralph Allen had joined us—and the films of the Film and Photo Section back to Reggio and then to Syracuse, where they were to be transmitted and flown to Algiers. Copy was transmitted, records were flown. On the ninth day of the campaign, the despatch rider was laid up with malaria, so we have to improvise our own methods of sending back copy, records, etc.

But better times were on the way. The despatch rider arrangements improved, the Army found more jeeps, and Alec MacDonald and the recording van caught up with the war.

And that was when war reporting complete with sound effects really began. The beauty of it was that the men could go forward with the portable, record their battle sounds, bring their discs back to the van and, with its facilities for cross-dubbing, do all the editing they wanted, intersperse commentary, and in fact produce a complete show. Sometimes they could get where they wanted by jeep, and run the portable on the jeep's batteries. The Italian roads were dusty in dry weather, though, and quite often the jeep could go only so far and they would carry the gear, with its own power supply, the rest of the way so as not to raise a dense cloud which would give away a position to the enemy.

The van had produced a notable programme before it reached Italy, the first Allied broadcast of "Lili Marlene." It was the brain-child of Peter Stursberg. "Lili Marlene," with its haunting melody and plaintive words, had been the song of Rommel's Afrika Korps in the desert war, and the British Eighth Army had appropriated it. They had been singing it a long while, but somehow no recording of it had ever reached the BBC or points west.

Stursberg heard some Italian peasants singing "Lili Marlene" in the fields around the villa on the slopes of Mount Etna where he and Alec MacDonald were staying while MacDonald waited for water-borne transport for himself and the van to the mainland. Straightway they went down in the van to Ionia, where they hired a local combination of five instrumentalists (none of them very good) and a singer to perform the song. The total fee was one pound. By the use of all its verses, interspersed with a historical commentary on the song, Peter put together a ten-minute programme. The BBC liked it so much when it reached London that they used it in their Home Service, thus drawing some letters of protest in London papers, including *The Times*. The writers who upbraided the BBC for broadcasting a Nazi song overlooked the fact that the Eighth Army had sung it from Alamein to Tripoli and then through Sicily, and was singing it still in Italy. Peter's commentary was apparently sufficiently clear to the Canadian audience, for there is no record of any similar protests against the CBC's use of the programme. In fact, the programme was included in a CBC museum of outstanding broadcasts.

Halton and Ouimet became sound addicts, recording barrages great and small, the talk of tank men over their radios during a battle, and the sounds of battle overhead. Marcel and Paul Johnson, by the simple expedient of parking the van on a hilltop between our guns and their target, made a programme that was not only heard in both English and French on the Canadian networks but was broadcast on all the BBC's services, home and overseas, was given the place of honour in "War Report," the fifteen-minute programme immediately after the nine o'clock news into which the BBC put the best material that had come in from any source, and excited Walter Winchell, one of the most widely syndicated columnists in the United States, to a paean of praise.

A barrage was being laid down by Canadian guns ahead of a Canadian infantry attack. Ouimet, standing beside the van holding a microphone while Johnson sat inside at the controls, could look back about a thousand yards to the gun positions and forward about two thousand yards to the town that was to be taken. In the valley between their vantage point and the town he could see the Canadian infantry moving forward behind the barrage. He had the wit to be silent—it was a novel idea in those days, when the average special events broadcaster seemed bent on a perpetual contest between his voice and the surrounding effects—and let the sound tell its story. It was all there, the gunfire, the whistling of the shells overhead, and the distant detonations as they exploded. To make things perfect, a few squadrons of spitfires roared directly over the microphone, by happy chance in the few intervals when the guns were silent. After it was all over he could intersperse narration, by means of dubbing, between the sounds.

The programme went by the Algiers route. Peter Stursberg, who was our man at AFHQ at the time, reported that practically all the correspondents in Algiers gathered in the studio to listen as it was relayed to London. In the United States the Mutual Network picked it up from the BBC's North American Service and next day, in New York, Winchell wrote for his millions of readers about "tanks rumbling by, Spitfires going overhead to the attack, Nazi and British shells whizzing by his ears," and went on to a graphic word picture of "the young Canadian correspondent standing his ground till the Nazis fled."

It hadn't been all that bad. The nearest Nazis were something over a mile away and retreating—although stubbornly—and the trajectory of the shells kept them safely above the level of Marcel's ears. And when he wrote about "British shells," Winchell had clearly overlooked Marcel's statement that the guns were Canadian. But he had got the basic idea: that this was a new way of reporting a war. The BBC introduced the programme as the finest recording of gunfire yet made. Next day one of the afternoon papers had a cartoon which showed a whole family diving under the furniture at the sound of "War Report."

The business did very nearly kill Johnson and Matt Halton. A request came from Canada for Halton to make a fifteen-minute programme on gunfire for inclusion in a Victory Loan broadcast. With Johnson he obliged. They set up the portable unit in a jeep, on the forward slope of a hill overlooking a valley and, across it, a corresponding hillside occupied by Germans. They chose the spot because it was an observation post for a shoot being put on by tanks. Halton ad libbed while the tanks fired and the German guns fired back, and the recording went along until a shell from a German 88 hit a tree close by them. The burst killed two soldiers in a slit trench a few feet down the slope, and sent Johnson sprawling across the hood of the jeep. The stylus skidded over the uncut portion of the disc. Johnson picked himself up and put on a new disc. Halton continued, and the Victory Loan campaign got its broadcast, the more dramatic for the interruption and Halton's explanation of it.

Later in the campaign Ouimet was ad libbing in French while a really big barrage from 2,400 guns was going over. He was at exactly the right distance from the guns for a perfect

pick-up. On impulse he said: "You fellows in Sorel who manu-
facture these twenty-five pounders, listen to them in anger," and
held up his microphone. Very soon afterwards he got a cable
from one of the Simard brothers, who owned the Sorel plant.
It said: "We have played your recording in the factory. You
have no idea of what it has done to boost morale."

Home in Canada after the war, Marcel met the sender of
the cable, who told him: "You don't know what the broadcast
meant to us. Our people were wondering what was happening
to those guns. They didn't realize until then that most of Montgomery's barrages were mounted with twenty-five pounders
from Sorel."

It wasn't all actuality. The greater part of the output consisted of reports spoken into the microphone. The voice of the
man who was there, transmitted so quickly through so many
stages from the battlefield to the living room, was still marvel
enough. But it was great to be able to record the sounds of
battle when that was the thing to do, or to give the listener the
actual voice and not merely the words of the man you were interviewing.

In mid-November Arthur Holmes and Lloyd Moore came to
the front to relieve Johnson and MacDonald. Halton's cable to
London announcing their arrival said they had had a "notable
experience" on the way. That was as far as censorship would let
him go. What had happened was that their ship, a converted
luxury liner carrying some thousands of troops and ninety-eight
Canadian nursing sisters, had been sunk by an aerial torpedo in
the Mediterranean. Surprisingly, there had been no loss of life.

Halton prevailed on Holmes to broadcast the story when the
censors allowed it:

The attack came in the evening, just as it turned dark. I was in the
dining room at the time, with Lloyd Moore of the CBC and Doug
Amaron of The Canadian Press, and about two hundred army officers.
The alarm calling the gun crews to their stations was sounded, and an
announcement was made over the loudspeaker that enemy planes were
approaching and all personnel were to stand fast. It wasn't long before
the guns of the convoy opened up and the German JU 88's made their
first run over. One of the waiters went on deck and quickly came back
to report that two of the German planes had been shot down and were

burning on the sea. About that time another waiter came running over to our table and shouted: "We got one." The words were no sooner out of his mouth then they got *us*. There was a terrific explosion which seemed to lift us out of our seats, and then the lights went out and the ship took a very sharp list to port. I was eating a piece of pie at the time, and seemed to have the impression that when I last saw it, it was floating in the air about on a level with my eyes.

Everybody immediately grabbed their lifebelts and felt their way to the doorway on the starboard side. I had foolishly left mine on a chair, and spent a few minutes finding it. When I did find it, the others had left and I couldn't find the door, but eventually I crawled over the wreckage and through a window on the port side, which was deserted due to the heavy list. I made my way aft to a clear deck, and was just in time to see the next attack on the ship. The planes were coming over at mast height, and as they came, all the guns in the convoy opened up on them with coloured tracers, shells and bullets. As they passed over our masts the guns all converged in my direction, and all those coloured tracers gave the impression that it was me and not the planes that they were shooting at. It was much the same effect as the type of fireworks at the Toronto Exhibition which seems to explode and come straight for you.

Everyone got off the ship safely and was taken on board another ship of the convey, from lifeboats and life rafts. Lloyd Moore and Doug Amaron, both good swimmers, were having a happy enough time in the warm Mediterranean when some people in a passing lifeboat decided to rescue them. Unfortunately Amaron's rescuer grabbed him by the ankles and hauled them on to the high gunwale of the lifeboat, which meant not only that he was plunged almost perpendicularly head downwards and half drowned before someone else hauled him in, but also that his beret came off and floated away with the two possessions he had managed to salvage—a packet of cigarettes and a pack of playing cards. He still doesn't know why he took the risk of going back to his cabin for those particular items.

Holmes, true to his calling as Admirable Crichton and the tradition of the merchant marine, worked hard at getting lifeboats away and helping nursing sisters into them. It was after four and a half hours of rowing that his turn came to climb a scramble net up the side of the rescue ship. "Feeling tired by this time from rowing," he said, "the climb up the net seemed to be about a thousand feet, with the top never nearer. It certainly was a great feeling to topple over the rail on to a solid deck again, where there was lots of dry clothing and hot coffee."

As progenitor and deviser of the portable–van tandem, Holmes might have permitted himself a few gestures of gratification at seeing it work so well. He didn't. It was no more than he expected of it. Instead he busied himself picking out sites for good sound pick-ups. A letter from him to a CBC internal publication, written around the end of 1943, survives in the files:

Before we took Ortona we brought our van to the village of San Vito to record a barrage and a battle. We parked the van beside a little church and as we were at a good elevation we were able to see the enemy's guns as they fired—and, incidentally, they could see us. But we got a good recording of the barrage, and when the Germans opened up we got a very good recording of their shells bursting close. These were their famous 88's and they come at you with quite a racket. . . .

About a week later we decided to move our billets into San Vito as the enemy had been driven back, and the town was only getting the odd shelling. We drove in about 5:45 pm and parked the van at the same spot where we had made our barrage recordings. Before unloading and getting settled we thought we would listen to the BBC news. We turned the radio on full and had the usual large audience of troops about. And what do you know? Half way through, the BBC announcer said: "We will now hear a CBC recording of battle sounds made during the recent fighting in Italy." Much to our surprise, the recording was the barrage and enemy shell-fire we had made at that exact spot a week earlier. . . . As you know, the BBC carries a large number of our shows. . . . Listeners might be interested to learn how far forward the CBC gets. It varies, but I can tell you that in some cases it would be impossible to get any closer without running into enemy lines. . . .

Recording difficulties are numerous and run to extremes. As Paul Johnson said, the summer heat made the discs almost too hot to handle. Now we find that we can hardly cut the discs as the cold makes them so hard, and low temperature produces high surface noises, too. . . .

Holmes and Moore had arrived as the Canadians were about to leave the hills of Central Italy to take part in the grand attack on the German winter line. So they were in time for the crossings of the Sangro and Moro rivers and the Battle of Ortona.

7–ORTONA

"Everything before Ortona was a nursery tale," said the 1st Division's commander after the battle.

"On a small scale it had all the ferocity of the Battle of Stalingrad," the official historian was to write later.

"The ante-chamber of Hell," was what Halton called Ortona while the battle was still on.

The battle for Ortona, a small town northeast of Rome, on the cliffs above the Adriatic, was the climax and finish of the greater battle of the Moro River. It lasted from December 20 to the early morning of the 28th. Halton described it as "a fit or convulsion of battle." While it was on, the broadcasts told of hand-to-hand fighting in which the attackers, having cleared one house, would blow holes through the walls to reach and kill the Germans in the next, room by room and floor by floor. When it was over, Halton said:

The Germans were demons: the Canadians were possessed by demons. The more murderous the battle, the harder both sides fought, from window to window, from door to door, in a carnival of fury. There was something different there, something heroic and almost super-human and, at the same time, dark as night.

They fought seven days and eight nights without rest, without sleep, amid fire and exploding mines and shells, and falling walls and thousands of bursting hand grenades, and always with the clattering of machine-guns—all this in a space of a few hundred yards.

The fighting rose in intensity as day followed day, and to

Halton's eyes was still gaining momentum on Christmas Day.
Yet to him and Ouimet the most memorable scene that day was
not of the fighting:

Christmas dinner in the shelled, broken church in Ortona. Candles and
white tablecloths. This was really a fantastic thing: not four hundred
yards from the enemy, carol singers, the platoons coming in in relays
to eat a Christmas dinner—men who hadn't had their clothes off in
thirty days coming in and eating their dinners, and carol singers singing "Silent Night."

Ouimet recorded the carol singers for his Christmas broadcast. The church's organ was part of the general ruin, but someone had found a harmonium, so the carols were accompanied.

The larger battle, the breaking of the German defences on
the Moro River, had gone on for two weeks before the Canadians reached Ortona, and had been ferocious enough. The daily
broadcasts were full of epic stories, among them that of the
heroic stand of the Royal 22nd Regiment (the Van Doos) at
Casa Berardi—although they were not allowed to identify the
regiment. When the battle was over, Halton told the stories
again in one broadcast—in condensed form, although it was a
long broadcast.

With the fall of Ortona, in the early morning of December 28th, the
Battle of the Moro River is over, and there is now a new name to add
to the list of great British deeds of the war.

Call them out: Dunkirk; Tobruk; Alamein; the delaying action in
Burma; Sidi Omar; the last stand at Sollum; the Battle of Tunis. Call
them out, and then add Moro River.

Measured on the scale of the last war, the Battle of the Somme, for
instance, or Passchendaele, or the enormous scale of the fighting in
Russia, this was not a big battle. But it was one of the biggest ever
fought by Canadians, and neither in this war nor the last, nor in any
other, has there been anything more bitter and intense. The attacking
Canadians beat two of the finest German divisions that ever marched,
killing them, man by man, in a long-drawn-out fury of fire and death
ending in the appalling week of Ortona.

The glory and the sorrow are not all Canada's because this was an
Eighth Army battle. British, New Zealand and Indian troops had
heavy enough fighting in the centre and on the left; but the main role
was assigned to Canada on the right flank, and the quality of this

battle on the right had something special that our race will never forget.

Halton went on to review the battle from its beginnings:

During November, British and Indian troops smashed the enemy's winter lines on the Sangro River. The enemy really thought he could hold us there throughout the winter. He had dug-outs and entrenchments of a kind not seen since the last war, and the Germans might be holding there yet except for our air support. On the Moro River, because of bad weather, we had no air support on a big scale. Moreover, the quality of the enemy troops on the Sangro was not what it was here.

And now the Canadians were brought down from the central mountains around Campobasso, where they had rested for several weeks, to take the right flank of the Eighth Army in its push for Pescara and the road to Rome.

On November 30th they were moving into action near the old town of San Vito on the sea. British engineers bridged the San Vito gorge for us under fire and every time we crossed it for the next ten days we were still under fire. The Canadians manoeuvred into position along the ridge overlooking the Moro River and on the night of December 6th we made our first attempt to cross that little creek. The Germans had rushed in their famous 90th light division of Panzer Grenadiers, to replace the beaten 65th infantry division and to meet the threat on the coast. The Canadians had to fight their way across the river at night to try and clear the enemy off the bank so that the engineers could build the crossings for the tanks and other supporting arms and supplies. There are two roads across, one a few hundred yards from the sea and another a mile to the left.

On the night of the 6th, an eastern Canadian unit crossed on the coast, and western Canadians on the right, but we were thrown back. On the right they attacked again with intense artillery support. Two companies got across, but the tanks could not get over to their support and they were pulled out under murderous fire, with losses. But at last light that day, a great officer took his men over again through a curtain of fire and the next morning, gallantly supported by British tanks, they made a desperate rush and took the high ground, and we were established across the Moro River.

Two of many great episodes of the crossing. "B" Company of a western Canadian unit, alone and surrounded across the river on the left, knocked out fourteen enemy machine-gun posts, an anti-tank gun and two tanks; and a field company of Canadian engineers built a log crossing over the river under steady small-arms fire as well as shelling.

The battle now focused on the village of San Leonardo on the crest just beyond the crossing. It was at this time that we captured a German document with the order: "The line of the Moro River is to be retaken and held, no matter what the cost in lives." In an action as close and ferocious as I have ever seen, two infantry units now tried to go through our bridgehead formations to take San Leonardo and the crossroads two miles beyond on the Ortona road. Our fine troops, our excellent men, burning for victory, and full of pride in themselves, made nearly twenty furious attacks, and every time the enemy counter-attacked through hundreds of his dead. The Canadians wiped the Panzer Grenadiers right out of existence, battalion after battalion of them, and then found themselves facing a still better German outfit, the 4th Parachute Division, a formation of savage, cunning young zealots as good as anything the warrior Germans ever produced.

The once-pleasant olive groves and vineyards and gardens on the slopes leading to the Ortona road became a bloody, churned up shambles. Our artillery laid down terrific concentrations of steel for nearly every attack we made and the Germans replied with the most artillery they have ever used against us, especially mortars and 88's, so that in a few days there was a shell hole wherever you stepped, and every tree was splintered, and not a leaf was left. Still the Canadians held and fought back. The Germans then were brave. The Canadians were heroic—remember they had to attack. Exhausted, lying and fighting in a quagmire of mud, with many of their comrades killed or wounded, their zest for the attack actually increased from day to day. Yard by yard, and German by German, they fought their way up to the crossroads to the hamlet of Berardi. Now our units were mixed up at times. Combat teams of tanks and infantry were formed and still the enemy would not give in. More than once I got forward to units in action, to see German machine-guns start shooting from behind us, and keep shooting until their crews were killed.

At last an eastern Canadian unit got into position to attack Berardi on the edge of a deep gully. Forty machine-guns awaited them, and they were counter-attacked by tanks. Then a fine Canadian unit attacked and was repulsed and surrounded, but it fought its way out and got to the crossroads. Once another unit was cut off for three days and when they fought their way out they could show a German document, announcing: "One of the most famous Canadian units is surrounded, and now will be totally destroyed."

Victory would have been impossible without the Canadian tanks, who provided our mobile artillery. Time after time, they advanced against enemy tanks and anti-tank guns to make a hole for this regiment or to come to the aid of another. One day a combat team was trying to cross the Ortona road, left of the crossroads. The group of tanks, under Captain Hugh Burns of Halifax, sent back a message advising that they could attack if necessary, though it would be suicide. The order came back, "We don't expect to see you again, but do it if you can." They did it—got two anti-tank guns with two lucky shots—and were seen again. Even with the taking of the road, the Germans wouldn't give up. They stayed on everywhere fighting in little pockets, and scores of them were killed in close action. Walking over the ghastly crossroads one day, we counted nearly two hundred dead.

Halton then went on to describe, in the vivid language already quoted, the grim story of street fighting in Ortona. He ended with these words:

At first light on the 28th, when I got to the command post of one unit, the colonel grinned, and said quietly, "I think it's over." A minute or two later a signaller jerked off his headphones and said, "Sir, the Jerries are gone, or else they are all dead."

He was to return to the battle in a retrospective broadcast from London a month later:

I sit here now in London, and at moments my memories seem like dreams; shadowy things which couldn't have happened. But at other times they are so vivid that I clench my fists. There was that first day, December 8th, when we got forward to a company of western Canadians who had just destroyed thirteen enemy machine gun posts in an afternoon. . . . There were the terrible rides back and forth across the Moro River and the San Vito Gorge. The infantry fights its way across a river first to make a bridgehead, and then the engineers build the bridges. Then the vehicles start moving, shells or no shells. At this minute, again I see a picture so vivid that I clench my fists: a convoy of ammunition trucks starting down the corkscrew road to the bridge. The Jerry gunners have every bend in the road taped, registered, and every few seconds they drop a shell here, and one here and one here, but the drivers have to go. When you run this gauntlet yourself, as we of the CBC often had to do four to eight times a day, it isn't so bad. There's an unholy thrill about it as well as fear. You are with good friends. You can laugh and joke. It's when you are watching others do it that you grow older, especially when a vehicle is hit and goes up in a vomit of flame and smoke.

There had been lighter moments. Holmes was with Halton

and Ouimet in the house to house fighting in Ortona, for no other reason than that it was going on. He certainly could not take recording gear into a house in which soldiers were blowing holes through walls to get at the Germans in the next house. In one house there was a large steel safe, which the soldiers, imbued with the spirit of dynamite, blew in. It was packed with bundles of 100-lire notes which cascaded to the floor. The men grabbed them up and stuffed them into pockets. Arthur stuffed a bundle into a breast pocket of his battledress. His fountain pen, in the same pocket, broke and spilled ink over the notes. He used them afterwards for playing poker, and left an ink-stained trail over a considerable area of Italy.

Holmes and Moore had found a source of innocent merriment one day before this, when Halton and Ouimet had decided to go to the front on their own. Investigating a captured German dugout somewhere on the Moro River front, they found a case full of parachute flares, some Very pistols, and a couple of bottles of wine. They took the lot back to the press camp. It was a fine afternoon, though chilly. They built a fire outdoors and opened the wine. After a couple of drinks they shot off one of the flares with one of the Very pistols. To their surprise it went off with a whistle and bang just like an 88mm. shell. They fired another, and more, at a rate that increased as the wine diminished. They had been at it a couple of hours when the lone correspondent in the camp emerged. The others were all away at the front but he had stayed back to catch up on his work. He had a shaken look.

"What a day!" he exclaimed. "I've just done a story on it. It's a wonder we haven't been hit."

A few days later Holmes and Moore volunteered to go in in the recording van and pick up the press camp's liquor ration. There was a long line-up in front of the stores building. They only had to fire off one flare—from behind a wall—to scatter the line-up and draw the camp ration without any waiting. On a more serious note, there was a ceremony to be recorded in the town square of Ortona when the battle was over and the rubble had been cleared away. The band of the Seaforth Highlanders— the same band that had played for the citizens of Agira in Sicily —played for the men who had won the town.

Then, while the Canadian units rested and refilled their ranks, Halton and Holmes went off on a quick tour of other elements of the Eighth Army—British, Indian, Newfoundland, New Zealand and African—gathering stories of battle and recording actuality. At the same time Ouimet went into hospital, where he stayed until the end of January. That left Lloyd Moore, the engineer, the only CBC correspondent in the press camp. Thus it fell to him to obtain one of the great actuality broadcasts of the campaign—a Requiem Mass, sung by members of the regiment, for the men of the Royal 22nd who had fallen in the Battle of the Moro River. Lloyd was at lunch in the mess when one of the public relations officers came in and casually mentioned that a Mass was to be sung at a church at Pontecorvo, some kilometres away. It was the first Lloyd had heard of it.

"When's it to be?" he asked.

"This afternoon," the officer said.

Lloyd rushed to the van and raced to Pontecorvo, getting to the church as the last men of the Van Doos filed in. Fortunately, the officers go in last at church parades. The adjutant saw him and came over, and at Lloyd's request asked the regimental chaplain not to start until he could get the recording gear running and a microphone set up. Then with microphone and stand in hand, and trailing cable behind him, Lloyd walked up the centre aisle of the crowded church towards the chancel steps. Two officers standing almost shoulder to shoulder in the front row partly blocked his way. He edged between them with an "excuse me," and got the microphone into position. As he turned to go back to the van, the two officers politely made way for him. They were General Montgomery and General Sir Henry Maitland Wilson, Allied Commander-in-Chief, the Mediterranean theatre. Ouimet came out of hospital to supply the introduction, linking commentary and closing, and the programme was away on the courier plane to Algiers and points west.

Halton flew back to London at the end of January, to be in plenty of time for the invasion of France. Before going, he broadcast a short review of the Italian campaign:

There is impatience at home, it seems, at the slow progress of the allied armies in Italy. What is the matter? Has the Eighth Army lost the spark which astonished the world?

The first answer is, if the public is surprised at the Army's slowness, the Germans are surprised at its speed. The Germans were quite confident that they could hold us all winter on the line of the Sangro River. They advertised the Sangro as their winter line. But the Army smashed this position. The German High Command then ordered their generals to hold us on the Moro River. The Army crossed the Moro River. The enemy was then told that the line must be re-established no matter what the cost in lives. That is the actual phrase. They paid a high cost in lives. Their dead are still lying there. But they re-established no line.

Yet it is true that our progress is slow. General Montgomery referred to this the other day in his farewell conference with war correspondents. He spoke of the mud and the mountains and the deep flooded valleys, and said that here in Italy there is no room for great strategem and decisive manoeuvre. Manoeuvre is the key word. In the desert, the attacking formation could go almost where it wanted. There was hardly any topographical limit to our freedom of movement. If we wanted to go somewhere, we went there, in a direct line, on compass bearing, with any number of vehicles abreast. But here we have to go on narrow mountain roads, full of craters blown by the withdrawing enemy.

I wish you could see the approaches to our Italian battlefield. The whole army has only three narrow roads along which to get at the Germans. Imagine a great army trying to manoeuvre along three narrow roads. Scores of thousands of vehicles have to keep moving backward and forward all the time, and this on these three roads, filing up and down the sides of deep gorges and over improvised bridges just wide enough to hold one vehicle, and probably under shell fire. There is one place where the engineers had to build five bridges over five demolitions in a space of four hundred yards; and there is the drenching cold rain, and the deep quagmires of mud.

If this army with its unsurpassed troops and its terrific fire power could manoeuvre, Rome would be ours soon enough. I do not say that the battle of Italy has been fought perfectly, but I don't know how any army could have fought harder or better—attacking a ferocious enemy under appalling conditions during the last few weeks.

Holmes followed Halton to London shortly afterwards. Benoit Lafleur came in from Algiers to take over the reporting for the French Network, but Ouimet stayed on to report in English till Peter Stursberg reached the theatre. He went back to London by ship early in March. It was an interesting voyage.

To begin with, Mount Vesuvius erupted as the ship drew away from Naples. It was a change from man-made explosions. His cabin mates were Captain Placide Labelle of Canadian Army Public Relations, Gregory Clark, the famous correspondent of the Toronto *Star*, and three American Red Cross officers.

"It didn't take Greg very long," he relates,

to get into conversation with a lady from the British Red Cross. When she saw that he was a Canadian, she said to him: "You might be interested, I was given a send-off party in Naples last night, and I was given some liquor, but I don't know what it is. I think it's called 'Canadian Club'."

Greg immediately said: "How much have you got?" She said: "A case, but I've never tasted the stuff."

Whereupon he picked up the case and brought it to our cabin.

There were about three hundred in the officer class in the ship. Every evening we used to knock off a bottle between the six of us in our cabin before dinner—the case just lasted the voyage neatly—and our British friends never understood how it was that all through the voyage these three Canadians and three Americans were so full of joie de vivre at dinner, because the ship was dry. We only told them on the last day of the voyage.

8–LONDON AGAIN

Being back in London did not mean being out of the sound of gunfire. London's air defences were vastly improved since the days of the Blitz, and the anti-aircraft guns, light, medium and heavy, could put up a fearsome barrage. The Blitz had ended in the spring of 1941, and there was to be nothing comparable to it until the summer of 1944 and the advent of the flying bomb, a terror that flew by day as well as by night and a noisome pestilence by either. But in the meantime the Germans had never left London alone for long. There were sporadic small raids during the rest of 1941 and through 1942. By the spring of 1943 the tempo of the raiding was increasing, and in the first months of 1944 the Luftwaffe was putting on what Londoners called the Baby Blitz. The guns kept the raiders high, and they were apt to drop their bombs on the "chuck it and chance it" principle, but they came in fair strength, up to 200 planes on some nights.

So things were noisy enough when Marcel came back to the flat in Harley Street that he and I had taken with Benoit Lafleur shortly after getting to London. Benny being still away, Matt Halton moved in and took his place for the last few weeks before D Day. Eighty-one Harley Street was a typical Overseas Unit address: stylish but top floor. When the bombing began, a lot of people who could afford to live in the West End found it advisable to move to the country, especially if they lived in upper flats. So a lot of formerly expensive accommodation was going at bargain rates. This was lucky for those of us who were liable to be at the office or in the studios till all hours and thus had to live within easy walking distance. During the Blitz, Arthur Holmes found it handy to have an apartment (which he shared with a succession of colleagues) in Portland Place, one of the stateliest thoroughfares in Marylebone. Against the advantages of its being cheap and within a few hundred yards of Broadcasting House were the disadvantages of its being thus in a prime target area and suffering a few grazing hits. Peter Stursberg fell on his feet into grandeur, at practically no cost, when he went to live with Wallace Reyburn, correspondent for the Montreal *Standard*, and two BBC men who occupied the whole top floor of an immense block of luxury flats, luxuriously furnished and also in Portland Place, for a grand total of ten pounds a week among them. John Kannawin lived on a top floor a few streets away. He had a flat to himself, but its door was always open to any member of the unit who happened to be temporarily without other accommodation. Others of us were dotted at a similar elevation around Marylebone, Westminster and Kensington. Our farthest outpost was Ma Pearce's, a crowded and happy-go-lucky boarding house in Bayswater, where the food was plentiful and where people who weren't subject to late hours at the office could live economically.

Our flat in Harley Street, though not as grand as Portland Place, had the advantage of being something better than top floor, being a sort of penthouse overtopping the adjacent roofs. If only it had had a few more windows we should have had a 360-degree view of the sky during air raids. Matt, who had slept beside the guns at Tobruk, rather groaned one night when I stuck my head in his room to suggest that he should get up and watch the fireworks, but he took an approving view of the defence nonetheless. His particular enthusiasm was the sight and sound of the rocket salvoes that filled the sky with jagged steel and trailing wires capable of shearing a wing off an aircraft. Marcel, although almost as inured as Matt by now to the sound of guns, did get up to watch with me that night.

It was always a spectacle worth watching: the blackout gone, the sky from zenith to horizon a constant winking of shell bursts; every so often a rocket salvo racing heavenward with an enormous "woosh" and looking, as it approached the top of its arc, like a huge bunch of red roses tossed across the sky, then exploding in a popping *feu de joie*. And, as the centrepiece for the whole scene, the brilliant illumination from a cluster of vari-coloured parachute flares dropped by the pathfinders and suspended over the target area (for some reason of security the censors would not let us mention the colours in our reports). It was also very noisy as the barrage rolled back and forth, the beat of the raiders' de-synchronized engines came from overhead and, now and then, bombs whistled.

Marcel and I once reported an air raid, very successfully and with sound, from our flat. We had not been saying much about the bombing in our broadcasts, since by 1944 it was an old story and the main interest at home was on the fighting in Italy, the coming invasion in the west, and our own vastly more destructive air offensive. But one morning we each got a cable, he from Montreal and I from Toronto, asking for a broadcast, with actuality, of the next suitable raid. It came a night or two later, and woke us up. We came out of our rooms simultaneously, wondering if it would do, and decided that it would if it lasted long enough for us to get dressed and on to the roof at 200 Oxford Street, some fifteen minutes' walk away. Then I re-membered that the roof microphone at 200 was always opened when a raid started, and telephoned the duty officer.

"Are you recording this one?"

He was.

"Can we have dubbings in the morning?"

"Certainly."

So we could watch from our own windows and get back to our beds as soon as the raiders had gone away. It wasn't one of the Baby Blitz's biggest efforts, but it had all the ingredients: the drumfire rolling back and forth, the raiders' engines, some bomb whistles and bursts; a lull in which a single gun seemed to be taking pot shots at a single plane; and a few rocket salvoes. The recordings the BBC handed us in the morning were a marvel of clarity. We chose our sounds, and prefacing each with an explanation, put together two highly instructive programmes, one in French and one in English, that were received at home magna cum laude.

Naturally we had our own various reactions to bombing. I am certain that I should never have wanted to go out with Arthur Holmes in the van during the real Blitz, but somehow during the Baby Blitz the roof at 200 Oxford Street seemed a secure enough place. Perhaps it was the steel helmet that one had to take with one's roof pass, and the microphone in hand that did the trick. On a night when the Underground was shut down because of a raid, a walk from Charing Cross to Oxford Circus, with shrapnel bouncing off the pavement, was hard on the nerves; but once on the roof and at work, all qualms departed, roar the barrage as it might. I remember one such night, though, when the duty officer who had given me my roof pass and steel helmet got home to his flat in Pall Mall to find it was no more—gutted, and every stick of furniture sucked out by blast from a stick of bombs that had fallen along the street.

I thought that Andy Cowan and I were overdoing things a bit on the evening he got back from North Africa in the fall of 1943. I met him at Euston Station, having dashed there from having a farewell drink with Art Holmes and Lloyd Moore, who were bound for Italy and for their rendezvous with a torpedo in the Mediterranean. The alert sounded as Andy and I walked from his railway carriage up the station platform, and the guns opened up as our taxi drove off. We had dinner at the French canteen, a pleasant place in St. James's Square that in its peacetime existence had been Lord and Lady Astor's town house. The barrage thickened as we ate, and there were occasional tremors in the floor. Thanks to double summer time it was still twilight when we had finished and got to the street door. The raiders were high and our heavies were chasing them, the sharp coughing of their air bursts punctuating the beat of engines. But Andy was a devotee of London and wanted to go for a walk and gaze on familiar sights. So we strolled out of St. James's Square into King Charles II Street, crossed Lower Regent Street and turned into the Haymarket, where Andy gave a detailed scrutiny to the theatre billboards. We talked about anything but the raid until he observed judicially:

"You know, this is interesting."

"What, in particular," I said.

"Oh, the whole thing. Here we are. You've just been seeing Art and Lloyd off to the Med, and met me coming back from the Med, and there's this going on up there."

I was grateful that he'd noticed.

Of course, we had the whole population of London for company in whatever dangers threatened from the sky, and we wouldn't have lived anywhere else. Our daily routine took us over famous thoroughfares: along Regent Street and down the Haymarket to Canadian Military Headquarters or Canada House just off Trafalgar Square; along Whitehall to the Houses of Parliament; along Holborn to Lincoln's Inn Fields where the RCAF had its headquarters; or into Bloomsbury, where the Ministry of Information and the press and censorship division of Supreme Allied Headquarters had their dwelling in a building that belonged to the University of London. Doing our best to live up to the milieu—although on our austere CBC salaries the effort pretty nearly broke us—we made the acquaintance, however fleeting, of most of the splendid hotels and famous restaurants, from the Savoy to the Dorchester and from Scott's to Quaglino's. As guests, we sometimes penetrated the mysteries of some of the stateliest clubs in Pall Mall. For the workaday round, there were a lot of service clubs and canteens where the food was cheap and the licensing hours accommodating. We had the best of two worlds in that we enjoyed the privileges of officers with the freedom of civilians. Not the least of the benefits from this dual status was that we were entitled to both civilian and military clothing coupons, a most useful consideration. All in all it was a good life.

And bombing or no bombing, the London office was a busy place. There were still entertainment programmes from Canada, like "The Happy Gang," being flown over on records for broadcast to the troops by the BBC. The original homeward bound programme "With the Troops in England" had been succeeded by "Eyes Front," which ranged over all the Canadian armed services and over all the fronts on which they fought as the war expanded. There were still concerts at camps and air stations. This volume of entertainment programming, together with the weekly newscasts for the troops, cabled from Canada, which he read at a machine gun pace, kept Gerry Wilmot in a state of perpetual motion which must have been unmatched anywhere in Britain. Paul Dupuis was almost as busy with his programme "Sur Le

Qui-Vive" for the French Network at home and the entertainment programmes and newscasts sent from Montreal for the French Canadian units.

There was a stream of regular or occasional speakers and commentators to be put on the air. Fred Griffin of the Toronto *Star* had a weekly spot until he went away to the front, as did Lionel Shapiro, once of the Montreal *Gazette* but overseas for the North American Newspaper Alliance, in the intervals when he wasn't at the war. Among our regular speakers, at one time or another, were George Darling of the BBC, in those days a political commentator, later to become a perennial M.P., a minister of state and a privy councillor; his Canadian colleague in the BBC, the incomparable J. B. McGeachy; from the Canadian Army Historical Section, Gerald Graham, before the war an associate professor at Queen's University in Canada, and after it, Rhodes Professor of Imperial History at the University of London; to speak on the war at sea, the naval correspondent of the London *Daily Herald*, A. J. McWhinnie, a tremendous authority whose eccentricity was to go to sea not in uniform but in the dark suit and homburg hat of the City business man, with rolled umbrella to match; and for a weekly review of the war in all theatres, a retired lieutenant general, Sir Douglas Brownrigg. Just now and then, a Canadian naval lieutenant would wander into the office with a script which he thought might be worth broadcasting and invariably was. He was Joseph Schull, whose book *The Far Distant Ships* is the official history of the Royal Canadian Navy in the Second World War.

The Canadian High Commissioner, Vincent Massey, was a frequent visitor. A less frequent but equally welcome one was Pierre Dupuy, who had helped Bushnell and Bowman with the French broadcasting authorities in Paris in 1940. After the fall of France the Canadian government had sent him first as minister to Vichy, and then to London as chargé d'affaires to the exiled governments there. There was a gentle stateliness about Mr. Massey's visits. The big chauffeur-driven car with diplomatic license plates would glide up to the Oxford Street curb decorously and well before the appointed time. Mrs. Massey would generally be with her husband and go down to the studio with him. Mr. Massey was a magnificent broadcaster and an impeccable writer, and any attempt to edit a high commissioner was improbable anyway, but he would always hand over his script for approval before he read it into the microphone.

Putting Mr. Dupuy on the air was different. He too was punctual, but he cut things fine. At the very last moment, as I paced the sidewalk beside the building, an apparently driverless Buick, painted in camouflage grey, would come hurtling down Great Portland Street like a projectile; Mr. Dupuy was his own chauffeur, he was short, and he liked to sit well down behind the wheel. The car would come to a sudden stop and the chargé d'affaires, having sprung out with a beaming smile and a "Hope I'm not late," would lead the way into the building in what must have looked like a spirited footrace.

There were variations from the London routine, if routine it could be called, though not all as interesting as the airborne adventures of John Kannawin and Harold Wadsworth. Kannawin had gone with Arthur Holmes to get some interviews with RCAF air crews in Coastal Command at a base in Northern Ireland. The job done, he was about to sit down to lunch when an officer rushed into the mess to tell him that there was a place for him aboard a Sunderland flying boat that was to take off in an hour. The station commander lent him his flying gear—"a formidable array of expensive equipment to risk on an amateur," he observed in his subsequent broadcast.

A methodical observer, he made note of his flying gear as he had done when about to fly the Atlantic in a Liberator:

There were three pairs of woollen socks and a turtle neck sweater, heavy fleece-lined flying boots and mitts, inner and outer flying suits held together, it seemed, by a mass of zippers and topped off by an earphone-and-microphone-equipped leather helmet, and the inevitable Mae West. I caught a glimpse of myself in the mirror, and had a momentary dim recollection of my modest childhood library, and a picture book about Robert Falcon Scott at the South Pole.

Kannawin's broadcast was carried in the BBC North American Service as well as over the CBC, and was later reproduced in the BBC publication *London Calling*.

We had been instructed to seek out enemy submarines and destroy them, or by our very presence keep them submerged during the night.

That would probably necessitate their coming up on the following morning, fair game for the daytime patrols. As I thought about the briefing I noticed the captain and the second pilot concentrating to left and right on the waters below. I looked forward and down and saw the tips of the front turret machine guns sweeping the low cloud above us and the sea underneath. . . . No-one was waiting to get to the patrol area. The submarine hunt was already on. If one was sighted, the Sunderland would dive on it, the front gunner would wipe out its deck guns and crew, and depth charges would be shot out and down on it. That is the recognized procedure, and often it works.

But we did not sight any submarines on our trip north west. Instead we sighted a large convoy inward bound to a United Kingdom port. We circled and wheeled around it to make sure that all was well. Below, the perfect lines of ships looked like child's toys in a bathtub, and surely they were almost as safe, for they were nearly home. But Coastal Command was on the job. Finally with a farewell bank and dip, we turned back on our course and the convoy melted into the grey union of sea and sky that formed our horizon. I felt a strange and justifiable thrill of joy, for I was in a Canadian-manned aircraft guarding these precious sea lanes without whose control Britain could not survive.

The Sunderland flew its patrol and got back sixteen and a half hours after take-off, without sight of a submarine. Kannawin's story would have been different if it had been the crew's next patrol and if he had got back to tell it. For on the next patrol the Sunderland did sight and dive on a submarine, and the submarine's answering fire killed the second pilot and wounded other members of the crew.

Wadsworth's adventure was in a bomber bound for Berlin on a night raid, the first mission of the first Lancaster to come off the production line in Canada. He flew with one of the portable units, as engineer for Ray Mackness, an RCAF public relations officer who had been before the war, as he was to be again when the war was over, a CBC announcer at Vancouver. Their Lancaster did not reach the target. Its engines were performing poorly and the aircraft, having lost height steadily on the outward run, had to turn back short of Berlin. It continued to lose height and ran the gauntlet of the enemy's anti-aircraft fire nearly all the way to the Dutch coast. Over Rotterdam it was so low that it flew between the cables of the balloon barrage. After practically skimming the waves across the North Sea, it crash-landed at its air station, damaged a hangar, ran on wild and eventually came to rest a few feet from a pile of rock that would have demolished it.

9–THE ROAD TO ROME

Peter Stursberg got to Italy at the beginning of March, with Joseph Beauregard as Holmes' replacement. There was not much doing on the Canadian front just then, so they toured the Ortona battlefield, and daily reports reminded the audience that though that battle was over, Canadian troops were still in the line and fighting, or busy at other tasks. They visited Canadian hospitals and rest centres, and found a group of Tito's Yugoslav partisans. At the end of April, Stursberg, Lafleur and Moore went to the Anzio Beachhead, which American and Eighth Army troops had been holding since January 22. At Anzio, Stursberg paid particular attention to Canadian members of the US First Special Service Force, a unit of picked men which was striking terror into the German lines by its skilful and daring patrolling. Anzio was only thirty-five miles from Rome, and the battle for Rome was in the making. But Moore was to report in a letter home: "We triumphantly entered Rome on June 5th, only to become back page news because of the D Day invasion."

By May 11 Stursberg and his colleagues were back from the beachhead and near Cassino to report the opening of the offensive which was to break the Gustav and Adolf Hitler lines and open the way to Rome. It was the beginning of a busy three weeks.

"It's now exactly twenty-five minutes past eleven on the night of Thursday the eleventh of May." Stursberg broadcast.

Twenty minutes after zero hour. And the sound that you hear is the opening gunfire of the great Allied offensive. Just listen to it. . . . [and

79

the sound of the guns came through] We are at a vantage point in the mountains near Cassino. It's dark now, but when we arrived here just before dusk we could see the ruins of the Benedictine Monastery quite plainly. . . . From here we also look down on the valley through which runs the famous Highway Number Six, the road to Cassino and to Rome. Across the valley is the Rapido River, which is the moat in front of the German Gustav Line.

I said it was dark—well, that's hardly right. The night is lit by the flashes of the guns. It's just as though hundreds of arc lights were flickering and sputtering, in the valley and behind the mountains too. The white flames bring the hills out in black relief. There's Mount Trocchio in a ring of fire straight in front of us. Sometimes it's so bright that I can see the CBC engineer, Lloyd Moore, bending over our equipment recording this. I can see him now as plainly as if it were daylight. . . .

Sheets of flame and balls of fire are leaping back and forth across the valley as battery after battery fires salvoes. It's an amazing and terrifying sight and yet thrilling. I don't know how to describe it properly in words, and I think it's easier for you to picture it by listening [more sound].

This is the greatest artillery action in the history of the Eighth Army—far greater than the famous barrage at El Alamein. There are guns in front of us—they're the ones that make the sharp cracks—and guns behind us—if you listen carefully you'll hear the whoosh of their shells going over our heads—and guns to the side of us. Literally thousands of guns are being used to-night.

That was the first of twenty-two reports, of varying duration, which Stursberg broadcast in the twenty-three days between the opening of the offensive and the entry into Rome. They covered the last stages of the battle for Monte Cassino, the breaking of the lines and the advance.

[May 12] Although it's a hot, sunny day, a deep swirling fog covers the Gari River where sappers and pioneers are working against time to repair the bridges so that our tanks can continue crossing. . . . We're at a forward headquarters of the Dominion armoured formation whose tanks were the first to break into the German Gustav Line. . . .

[May 13] Smoke hangs over the Liri Valley, hiding the glorious green mountains on either side from the tired eyes of our soldiers. The Germans are fighting fiercely as everyone expected them to do—clinging stubbornly to the Gustav Line as though it were a bastion of the Reich. . . . At no time in the war so far has the Eighth Army had so many guns—and the Eighth Army is very fond of artillery. The gunners at one medium battery which I visited told me that they'd fired more shells during the last two days of the offensive than they'd fired in all the months that they'd been in Italy. . . .

[May 14] It's difficult for me to describe the grim struggle that is going on in the mountains above Cassino. I've just heard about it from the men who have been there and fought and suffered there—and now that I come to tell the story I realize how inadequate words are. There's no possible way that I could exaggerate the hardships of this terrible battle, and I'm only afraid that I won't be able to make them sound real enough. I can still see the strained look on the faces of the men who had come out of those hills of Hell behind that satanic monastery. . . .

[May 17] The haze of battle covers the gently rolling fields of the Liri Valley like an early morning mist. It lifts a little and we can see the German mortar shells bursting on the road ahead, but never enough to see the monastery above Cassino which is only a few miles away. . . . Everyone seems in a hurry at the advance headquarters, but some drivers are sitting under a tree trying to relax and talk amid the din of the guns. One of them says: "I hear we got Cassino," and another turns to me and asks: "What's this I hear about the second front starting today?". . . .

[May 23] The attack on the Adolf Hitler Line has begun. Canadian infantrymen and Canadian and British tanks are now storming its outer defences. Our troops are being supported by one of the heaviest artillery concentrations of this war. Hundreds of guns have been massed in the Liri Valley here for this attack, which is on a very narrow front. Just listen to those guns roar. . . . We're in the attic of an old Italian farmhouse that overlooks the front. . . . Not all the shell fire's on our side; the Germans are replying but their crumps are some distance away and I doubt if you can hear them above the noise of our guns. . . . Our infantry and tanks should now be assaulting the Hitler Line. The Canadians have been given the hard part of it to crack. The barbed wire in front of the pill boxes and bunkers is said to be twenty feet thick. . . .

[May 24] It's strangely quiet in the Liri Valley now that the Canadians have broken through the Adolf Hitler Line. Only yesterday it was hideously noisy here and the ground shook to the crash of the guns, and smoke hung heavily over the land. Now it's like a summer day in the country, with the fields warm and fragrant and full of promise. . . .

[May 26] It's becoming a mad chase in blinding dust over bumpy mud roads to keep up with the Canadian advance now. For instance, today it took us nearly three hours to reach an armoured formation headquarters, only to learn that our forward elements were still miles away. . . .

[May 27] I have just flown over the Liri Valley and seen the Germans retreating down the road to Rome. A British Army pilot took me up in a light plane that's used as an air O Pip [observation post] for the guns, and I was able to look down on the battlefield between the Melfa River and Ceprano. It was one of the most thrilling experiences of my life; and yet it didn't seem real somehow, and I had to make myself believe that the red flashes in the mountains were German guns firing, and that those little black beetles crawling down below were Canadian tanks advancing. . . . Before we took off, the pilot said: "You know we're a sitting duck for enemy fighters. But I haven't seen many of them around for a long time." . . . I got Captain Wright to fly low over the monastery, and had the best view of its tragic ruins. From the air the monastery looked like a broken box half full of rubble. Parts of the great walls still stood, but inside there was nothing but heaps of stone. . . . The battle beyond the Melfa River—and the enemy movement down to Ceprano—all that seemed unreal from the air, but the old battlefield of Cassino looked much more stark when we looked down on it from the plane. It was like a scabrous sore on the face of the earth. . . .

[May 29] There are many rivers to cross along the road to Rome that the Canadians are taking. The Gari and Rapido, the Melfa and the Liri—we're over them now—but there are others farther on, others that will have to be bridged by our engineers. . . .

[May 31] Some idea of the speed of this advance can be gathered from the fact that one medium artillery regiment did its shooting while on the move. The guns were deployed in the fields but their fire was controlled from vehicles on the road. . . .

[June 3] We're with the Canadian tank brigade whose charge across the Liri Valley and over the Melfa River put the Germans to such rout that now our forward echelons are rolling along Highway No. 6 meeting little or no opposition. The tanks are in harbour now and their crews are enjoying a well-earned rest. The colonel of the western Canadian tank regiment which led this great charge is sitting on the steps of his caravan. He looks tired and his arm is bandaged where it was cut by shrapnel during the action, but he's a proud and happy man. . . . The time set for the crossing of the Melfa River was three days. This tank regiment reached the Melfa in little more than a couple of hours, and a crossing was made that afternoon.

The next day, June 4, found Stursberg with the Americans as they reached the outskirts of Rome. For the occasion, the United States Army set up a high-powered radio transmitter in a truck on the highway, and allowed the correspondents a few minutes' air time each. Thus Peter, for the only time it happened in our battlefield reporting, got out a broadcast that went direct to Canada without recording or relay.

It was all tremendously important, and all overshadowed by the imminence of the invasion of the west. The Allies entered Rome on the day before D Day, and thus a long-awaited triumph did become back page news. But Rome did afford Benoit Lafleur a coup in the form of a broadcast to Canada, or rather two broadcasts, one in French and one in English, by Pope Pius XII. It was the first time His Holiness had ever broadcast over any other station than the Vatican Radio, and the first time he had ever broadcast in English.

It took complicated negotiation, and Lafleur afterwards gave the credit to a young Italian named Marcello Dussio who had attached himself to the Royal 22nd Regiment so successfully that he was allowed to wear the uniform of a Canadian officer with one pip and thus enjoy the unusual rank of *sous-lieutenant*. Dussio, a man with contacts, introduced Benny to the papal chamberlain, and the chamberlain took the matter up with the Pope. At first the word came back that the Pope would broadcast in French only, but Benny, who had asked for an English version too, asked again and was rewarded. It was unfortunate that static over the Atlantic conspired with the Pope's pronunciation to make the English broadcast unusable, but the one in French was a great success.

Lloyd Moore was at the controls in the van parked below while the Pope spoke from his study. With him in the study His Holiness had a live audience consisting of Lafleur and the CBC engineer Joseph Beauregard, the papal chamberlain, Lt. Colonel Jean Allard of the Royal 22nd, and the unofficial *sous-lieutenant* Marcel Dussio.

There came a sequel when Lloyd Moore got a cable from Engineering Headquarters in Montreal instructing him to ship immediately the microphone the Pope had used. This presented a difficulty. The microphones we used at the front were handsome things, having been specially designed for the Canadian royal tour of 1939, each of them surmounted with a crown. But they all looked alike. Every recording van carried several, and when not in use they were stored together in a box. Lloyd had not a clue as to which of his stock he had set up in the Pope's study. Lafleur, Beauregard and Stursberg were all sitting in the van with him, helping him ponder, when he had his inspiration. Shutting his eyes, he plunged a hand into the microphone box and drew out the first one he touched. Holding it out before his audience he opened his eyes, gazed on it reverently for a space, and announced: "This is the microphone through which His Holiness broadcast to Canada."

So they sent it to Montreal by parcel post.

10–D DAY AND V BOMBS

"There's something in the air!" Matt Halton had said in a programme, a sort of radio tour of London, that we sent home on Easter Sunday. It opened with a parade of Canadian First World War veterans marching along the Mall to the music of a Guards band, for Easter Sunday in 1944 was April 9, the anniversary of the Battle of Vimy Ridge. Farther along in the programme was talk in Trafalgar Square with Canadian soldiers in town on what looked like their last leave before the invasion.

There was indeed something in the air that spring, in every camp and seaport, in every London street, and very noticeably in the Overseas Unit office where we strove with preparations for the coming day. The plans for reporting the invasion were as elaborate, on their own scale, as those for the invasion itself. There was a multiplication of press conferences and briefings, and of directives from various high quarters, labelled as to their varying degrees of secrecy. The BBC had been made the clearing house for all the broadcasting agencies, and had set up two war rooms to receive and distribute incoming reports; one at Broadcasting House for transmissions by radio and one at the Ministry of Information for recordings brought in by courier plane and despatch rider. For correspondents sending written copy there were to be, for the first days, soldiers wearing identifying armbands at all the south coast ports where ships returning from the beachhead would come in, to receive any despatches that had been put on board and rush them to the nearest telegraph station. The BBC would operate, on behalf of all the broadcasting agencies, a four-kilowatt radio transmitter which the army was to put up as soon as the beachhead was secure. For us in the Overseas Unit there was the particular preoccupation of having the recording gear ready and in the right places: the portable in a jeep at Southampton, to cross the Channel within a few days of the landing, and the van somewhere back in the marshalling line, to follow as soon as the traffic would allow.

The correspondents who were to land with the Canadians were objects of special attention and solicitude to their friends. And knowing what they did about the West Wall defences, they had reason to be a rather thoughtful lot. I remarked one day to Matt Halton, who of course was one of the elect, that where two or three D Day correspondents were gathered together there was bound to be a prayer meeting. Matt thought well enough of it to put it in a broadcast.

"It's going to be no picnic for Marcel and Matt and the other correspondents who go in early," I wrote to Dan McArthur in a review of our arrangements on May 15. "I've never seen such a serious-minded bunch of young men as the corps d'élite of the war correspondents, as they are at present. Not edgy, just a trifle wistful, and I don't wonder."

Lionel Shapiro talked with gloomy satisfaction, one fine Saturday afternoon about that time, as we walked along Upper Regent Street from the studios, of his chances of being killed on the beach. He found the topic absorbing as he walked head down and hands in pockets, and took no notice as a group of three American officers, a captain, a major and a very tall colonel, approached from the opposite direction. This was unfortunate, since American officers were punctilious about saluting anyone in an Allied uniform with unfamiliar rank badges, and while I was in civilian clothes, Lionel wore an intimidating outfit: an officer's forage cap with the green band that denoted a British war correspondent; a battledress tunic with flashes saying "Canadian War Correspondent" and the large and eye-catching shoulder patches of the U.S. 5th Army, of which he was proud because General Mark Clark himself had presented them to him at Anzio; and a pair of the U.S. Army slacks known as pinks. The inevitable happened. He interrupted himself to ask, a few paces on: "Did that American colonel salute me?"

"Yes, Lionel."

"Too bad." And he returned to the mounting odds.

The D Day correspondents were likely to be of interest to enemy agents as well as to their friends. The sudden and simultaneous absence of a lot of well-known correspondents from their offices or their accustomed pubs would be a good invasion tip-off. So several times during the month or six weeks before D Day they were summoned to report, with full kit and every appearance of readiness to go abroad, at some secret rendezvous in London whence they would be conveyed to another and equally secret place somewhere in the country. On one of these exercises they met General Montgomery. When he joked about their being "the assault wave of the war correspondents," their laughter was as much from politeness as from amusement. If these sorties interested enemy agents as much as they did our landlady in Harley Street when Matt and Marcel were away on them, they must have given the German intelligence a lot to think about.

But the morning came when Matt Halton strolled into my office with the words: "I can't say anything, but . . . ," and while the pause still hung on the air, Marcel Ouimet followed him in, looking impressively nonchalant. They had both just received the telephone calls telling them that they must leave and that this was the real thing. They had to go home and pick up their gear, and the flat being a better place for farewells than the office, we all three walked around to Harley Street, where we made the pleasing discovery that there was enough left in our several bottles for a couple of ceremonial drinks around. They descended to the street one at a time, because one correspondent plus bedroll, pack and other gear, filled the floor space of our small elevator. On the street a specially ordered taxi was waiting. It would have been more convenient if they could have had a jeep sent from CMHQ, but Security had said "No." A jeep at a correspondent's front door would be too likely to attract attention.

Nine correspondents went ashore with the Canadians on D Day. They were Ross Munro and William Stewart for The Canadian Press; Ouimet and Halton for the CBC; Ralph Allen of the *Globe and Mail*, chosen by lot to represent the combined Canadian daily newspapers; Lionel Shapiro for the North American Newspaper Alliance; Charles Lynch for Reuters'; Ronald Clark for the British United Press, and Joseph Willicombe for the International News Service. They were not landed with the first assault waves, so they escaped the storm of machine gun fire that met the first troops and cut down so many men before they could cross the beaches. The plan was that they should go ashore an hour after the initial assault, though in some cases the congestion of landing craft and the fierceness of the resistance on the beaches lengthened this interval. They were landed, with their conducting officers, at various points along the Canadian sector, and went their ways singly or in pairs until the next day, when they made rendezvous at Courseulles and set up their first press camp.

Halton, the veteran from North African days, went ashore at Graye-sur-Mer with Charles Lynch, aged twenty-four and seeing his first battle. It was the beginning of a lifetime friendship. Lynch recalls that they and their conducting officer, Captain Placide Labelle, spent their first night of the invasion in great comfort, welcomed into a French farmhouse and sleeping between sheets. Ouimet, having spent the night before the invasion on board a Royal Navy frigate with Ralph Allen—he recalls that the accommodation was most comfortable—landed at Bernières-sur-Mer with the Régiment de la Chaudière. The Chaudière were the reserve battalion of the 8th Brigade.

It was some two hours after the first landings when Ouimet got ashore, and the fire on the beach had mostly died down. There was shelling from German 88's inland and from heavier guns, as yet unsilenced, in the shore fortifications, but very little small arms fire. Nevertheless, he typed his first despatch sitting on the beach with his back to the sea wall. It seemed a sensible precaution. He also wrote it soaking wet. The business of getting ashore had been one that dwells with him yet.

On one of their pre-invasion expeditions, the correspondents had been instructed in the way to invade: the thing in leaving a landing craft was to go down the ramp and jump into the sea in two's, hand in hand, so that if one man got knocked over by a wave or the backwash of a passing vessel, the other would be able to support him till he found his footing. Marcel went in carrying his typewriter in his left hand and holding the hand of his conducting officer, Captain Bill Cornforth, in his right. The only trouble was that the water was deeper than they had expected, up to Marcel's chest, and that Cornforth, a much shorter man than he, stumbled as they went forward.

"For some seconds after we had set foot on bottom," Marcel recalls, "the only thing I saw was the top of a steel helmet advancing over a wave. When we'd got a few paces forward and his head emerged, salt water was coming out of his ears, out of his nose, and out of his helmet."

Their uniforms had to dry on them, since there was no room for spares on an amphibious venture of this sort. An annoyance that somehow rankled in Marcel was the damage to his best pair of tan boots, purchased at great expense somewhere in Jermyn Street. He had put them on in a mood of fatalism. The correspondents had been told that a casualty rate of 20 per cent. was expected in the landings. Applied to the nine correspondents, that meant the likelihood that one and three-quarters of a war correspondent would be hit. If he was to be either the one or the three-quarters, he wanted to be respectably dressed.

The flatness of the terrain was a bit disconcerting at first. In Italy there had generally been some natural protection like a large boulder or a small hill behind which one could set up the recording equipment or sit down to type a story. The flat fields of Normandy, where the wheat was not yet tall enough to provide even the illusion of cover, seemed to provide the enemy with a very fair field of fire.

"I suppose it was only an impression," Marcel says, "because when we were in the villages we could always get behind a solid stone wall when things got hot."

While the chosen nine went ashore, other correspondents were filling assignments of their own. Andrew Cowan, deprived of the job he wanted—a run in on one of the first assault landing craft—was confined instead to a troopship from which he saw the men of the Winnipeg Rifles transfer to their landing craft and go in at Courseulles, and also saw the first wounded brought back. Bill Herbert was at Ford Airport on the English south coast, from which No. 403 Spitfire squadron of the RCAF—the Wolf Squadron—was providing part of the fighter cover for the landings. But it is doubtful if any of them had an experience to match that of the CBC's unofficial correspondent Don Fairbairn.

Fairbairn had accepted the place for what we thought was

to be an observation flight over the beaches as the landings began. It turned out to be a mission to bomb one of the River Orne bridges some thirty miles inland, in conjunction with the airborne landings which preceded the assault from the sea. Some time after midnight of June 5-6 he took off from an airfield in Kent, in one of a squadron of Mitchell bombers. The correspondents—and Corporal Fairbairn of RCAF Public relations enjoyed correspondent status for the occasion—were the only men aboard the planes who knew that this was D Day. After the crews had been given their briefing on their objectives, the correspondents were taken aside and told more: of the seaborne invasion and the airborne operations that were under way. And they were told not to tell the crews they were flying with.

It was a long route and one that kept them airborne for some six hours: the first leg far up the North Sea before the squadron turned back to head for the invasion area. Over the French coast Don's plane got lost, perhaps understandably since it was the navigator's first operational flight. It missed the bridge it was supposed to bomb and flew over Caen, where it came under intense anti-aircraft fire and had its starboard engine knocked out and the port engine so damaged that it took them home running at a third of its proper oil pressure, and its hydraulic system and its radio also knocked out. The aircraft turned for the Channel, losing altitude. On the way to the coast, the crew proposed dumping the bomb load as soon as they reached the Channel, and Don had to restrain them. He was still bound by his pledge of secrecy, so all he could say was: "Wait till you see what's underneath you."

The plane cleared the cliffs of Dover by a hundred feet or so. To add a final touch, some of our own coastal anti-aircraft guns opened fire on it but fortunately it was too low to be hit. It staggered back to its airfield but it never flew again. The crew made a rapid count of shrapnel holes on landing. There were about 110 of them.

For Ouimet and Halton D Day was the start of a campaign that was to keep them almost uninterruptedly in the field until they got to Berlin nearly a year later. Cowan, after D Day, was to have a spell in motor torpedo boats hunting enemy shipping in the channel, then sail again to the French coast in a Canadian destroyer escorting components of "Mulberry," the prefabricated dock system that gave the beachhead an artificial harbour; report the bombardment of Cherbourg from the deck of the Royal Navy cruiser *Glasgow*; sail on the old battleship *Warspite* in its last engagement before it went to the scrap yard—a bombardment from the sea in support of the Canadians in the battle of the Falaise Gap; and contrive to be in Cherbourg on the day that General de Gaulle landed there.

In London, the long beleaguered fortress and the nerve centre of the invasion, the coming of D Day was almost anti-climax. There had been the awaited telephone calls to the head-quarters correspondents on the previous evening, summoning them to an early morning conference in the SHAEF (Supreme Headquarters, Allied Expeditionary Force) Information Room at the Ministry of Information. The Information Room was crowded, and when the communique announcing the start of the invasion had been read there was a rush to the telephone booths. But there was no surprise.

Strangely emptied of uniforms, London seemed almost remote from the war. The spectacle of the buses rolling unconcernedly along Regent Street and Oxford Street was at odds with the realization that the battle for civilization was being joined a hundred and fifty miles away. The sense of remoteness was of course illusory, and would be banished completely by the arrival of the flying bombs a week later. And no such interval was allowed the Overseas Unit staff in London, for whom battle was joined, before the first salvoes fell on the enemy-held beaches—with accident and with the multiple plagues that can beset a complicated communications system.

For one thing, the recording equipment was late getting over, despite all the precautions taken by us and the army. It was a good thing that the beachhead transmitter was at work without delay. Then confusion blossomed, briefly but unbelievably, at the key forwarding points, so that recordings disappeared from human ken in the brief transit from the BBC war room to our studios, and cabled despatches went irrecoverably to earth some-where in the mazes of MOI and SHAEF. It took round-the-clock toil to get our beachhead reports out across the Atlantic during the invasion's early days. In the beachhead, the correspondents were always within range of enemy fire: from artillery and snipers by day, and from bombers by night. They were shelled out of one of a succession of press camps, with great loss of equipment but, remarkably, no loss of life. The shelling set the building on fire, and destroyed all of Ross Munro's equipment, along with that of Lionel Shapiro, and Ross's Canadian Press colleague Bill Stewart; Halton and Ralph Allen managed to save some of theirs. Ouimet missed the shelling—and vice versa—since he was away at the front when it happened. He reported his losses as comparatively slight, but his indent for replacements was enlightening as to the requirements of a well-equipped war correspondent. First he needed a cable sent to Montreal for the prescription for his glasses. His message continued:

From London perhaps you fellows could send with the van a water bucket. They can be had at Gore's. Also some hair brushes, shoe brushes—black and tan—and shoe polish. Also if you have a spare safari bed would appreciate your sending it over. My bed escaped but it has a few holes in it from catching on fire. Oh yes, and I would need a binocular case. If you can, send us some paper and carbon as well. I haven't had a shave in two days because I lost all my toilet articles. It was quite a show, I am told, but am not sorry to have missed it. This war is a hard war to cover. Much more difficult than Italy, but we are doing our best. . . . Both need cigarettes badly.

The recording van, with the water bucket and the rest of the gear, and best of all with the belated portable unit on board, reached the beachhead, with Alec MacDonald as engineer. The shelling of the beachhead press camp came exactly a week after D Day. It was also exactly a week after D Day that the first flying bomb fell on London.

The flying bomb, or V-1 (for *Vergeltungswaffen* 1, the plural of First Vengeance Weapon), was a small pilotless airplane. In its nose it carried 2000 pounds of high explosive. Its range was just under two hundred miles, its speed close to 400 miles an hour, it generally flew at about 2,000 feet, and these statistics are unquestionably relevant to the story of the Overseas Unit. The noise made by a V-1 in flight can only be described as deplorable, and the explosion on impact was shattering. The bomb carried a controlling mechanism by means of which, when it had travelled its predetermined distance, it was pushed over into a steep dive which cut off the fuel supply and stopped the engine. The only good thing about it was that the dive generally took thirteen seconds, so that from the cessation of its engine sound, people in the vicinity had those seconds to take cover. Occasionaly though, the mechanism would fail and a V-1, having used up its fuel, would simply glide aimlessly, losing height gradually, instead of diving. It was a ghostly experience to hear one of these wild V-1's pass low overhead with the wind singing over its surfaces.

The flying bomb caused devastation enough, but it might have been infinitely greater. If it had been the surprise that the enemy intended, and launched as early and in as great numbers as he intended, it might have changed the whole course of the war. It is horrifyingly easy to imagine what would have been the effect, a month or two earlier, of a sudden drenching of embarkation ports, troop assembly areas and other vital points with a totally unexpected long-range bombardment of tremendous destructive power and the capacity for prolongation until its work was done.

It was one of the great deliverances of the war that Allied intelligence had got word of a new long-range weapon as early as April, 1943. By August of that year the Air Force was bombing the V-1 experimental station at Peenemunde, though at great sacrifice of life, and thus striking at the heart of Hitler's great enterprise. In the months that intervened before the invasion, innumerable sorties were flown against the launching sites that the Germans were installing along the French coast. They too entailed great sacrifice of life, but the sacrifice purchased time in which to develop a defence, delayed the attack until our first troops were ashore and enlarging their beachhead in France, and reduced the bombardment to far less than its intended weight.

Hearing the first flying bomb was something I shared with a few million other people, but I have always felt a proprietary interest in it because it sounded as if it was coming right through the roof of 81 Harley Street. It was late at night. The air raid alert had sounded, itself a surprise because the raids had stopped weeks before. Then almost immediately came a puzzling noise from a single aircraft. The initial idea that the night fighters must be very low was immediately banished, as the noise grew into a deafening crescendo, by the conviction that it was a plane in a bombing dive. Then whatever it was, it was gone. Local officials were even more puzzled after an unidentifiable aircraft crashed on some railway tracks south of the Thames, with an explosion that did a lot of damage. At the Ministry of Information next morning it was still a puzzle. At a second press conference later in the day we were told that Hitler had released a new weapon and that things were going to get serious.

They didn't come in any great numbers the next two nights, but on the Saturday night the pace stepped up, and from the front windows in Harley Street they seemed to be trundling in procession, visible by the flaming exhaust gases coming out of their tails, up Portland Place, though they were probably farther away than that. One of them got hit by an anti-aircraft shell and went up in a flash and a roar. It was extremely foolish to be standing pressed against the window, although fortunately it was open top and bottom. Always after feeling the rush of air that came in with the force of a blow, I tried to stay away from windows when flying bombs were coming.

When the defence got organized it included interception by aircraft over the Channel, and between the coast and London a combination of fighter interception, anti-aircraft gunfire and balloon barrages. There was no shooting at them over London. But for the first nights the London guns went after them furiously. If one was abroad, out of doors, it was disconcerting to have a lot of gunners trying to shoot down over one's head tons of high explosive that were heading for somewhere else.

From that first Wednesday night after D Day, flying bombs continued to hit London almost to the last weeks of the war, but the period of the most intense attack was from June to the end of August, 1944. In that time the Germans launched some 8,000, of which 2,300 reached the London area. Anyone who was in London for any of that time might well imagine the number to have been much larger. After a night in which they had seemed to stream over unendingly, in a series of approaching crescendos and shattering explosions, it was a surprise to go out in the morning and see the surrounding buildings still standing. But for many people the morning surprise never came. Between June 13 and August 31 flying bombs killed nearly 5,500 people, injured another 16,000, and destroyed or damaged more than a million dwellings, mostly in greater London. They came over at all hours, for daylight or darkness made no difference to them.

A rather maddening restriction on our reporting of the V-1 bombardment was that censorship would not let us say that it was falling on London. "Southern England" was as close as they would let us come. When we broadcast home a perfect flying bomb recording—the crescendo of the approach, the thirteen seconds of the silent dive after the engine cut off, and the roar on impact—we had to say it happened "in southern England" when the recording had been made by the simple expedient of hanging a microphone out of an office window. And it grew irritating to get letters from friends at home who were glad it wasn't London that was being bombarded. It was not until July 6 that Mr. Churchill, by giving the House of Commons a review of the flying bomb attack, lifted security and released the real story. The security was so good that Lloyd Moore, returning to London from Italy soon after D Day, was completely taken by surprise by his first flying bomb. He was in a taxi on his way to the office from Paddington Station when a thunderclap of an explosion sounded close by. There had been no alert, and there was no barrage going up, and he came into the office demanding to know what was going on.

He was familiar enough with flying bombs by the time, a few days later, he was recording for the BBC a message from King Haakon of Norway to the Norwegian people. The King was speaking from his study while Lloyd sat at the controls in the van parked below in the street. It was a message of encouragement, telling of the success of the invasion and the inevitability of Germany's defeat. The King had just told his people that the day of their liberation was approaching when a V-1 went off near enough to send the needle skidding. In the pause while Lloyd hastily put on a new disc, the King remarked to him over the line:

"Doesn't sound much as if we're winning, does it?"

The main flying bomb attack was to end with the clearing of the coast across the Channel and the overrunning of the launching sites, though there was to be a resumption, on a much smaller scale, with V-1's launched from bombers over the North Sea. But before that resumption, the next terror weapon, the V-2, would be launched against London.

11–NORMANDY

On June 20 Halton was reporting:

The Battle of France is now nearly two weeks old, and we are firmly established. The foothold is still small; the Germans strong and ferocious, and vast issues still hang in the balance. Terrific battles still have to be fought before we secure Northwestern France and break through towards Paris and flush the Germans out of France. But we are here. It will be some months before the full story of the Third Canadian Division can be told. The names of its regiments— some of them already famous, some of them to become famous in a few days— cannot yet be mentioned. We still can't describe what each unit did in what area, or how such a unit went on fighting in such a village after long and murderous days when much of its strength was gone. But I'll tell you what I can.

These men were new to battle. They'd never heard the screaming shrapnel before. They hadn't been machine-gunned or sniped at. They hadn't had bombs thrown in their faces. They hadn't been overrun in their slit trenches by tanks. But they have now, and they know that there are no better fighting men on earth.

By the night of D Day, the Canadians had taken nearly all their objectives, and that night, already, the conquest of Germany had begun. Of all the Allied infantry assault forces, a brigade of western Canadians was the only one to take all its objectives and hold them against every attack ever since. And what ferocious attacks they were: The German storm troops included the 21st Armoured Division, famous in the old desert campaign, and the 12th SS Hitler Youth Division, a formation of cunning and ferocious young Germans who'd been indoctrinated since childhood with the most fanatic Nazism and with only one idea—to fight like devils and throw us back. That's what the Canadians faced on the first night and every hour through the next bloody three days. That was their initiation into the horrors of war, but they never budged.

One of the first important operations in the breakout from the beachhead was the Canadians' capture of Carpiquet village on July 4. Halton and Ouimet, with Alec MacDonald as engineer, watched and recorded the battle from a forward observation post. It was a memorable battle, and so were the broadcasts. Here is Halton's opening:

It's two minutes to five. Two minutes to five in Normandy, and the sun hasn't risen yet, over us or over the Germans eight hundred yards away. It will rise on a fearful scene, because at five o'clock precisely, the Canadians are going to attack. And they'll attack with the most enormous concentration of fire ever put down on a small objective. The morning is as soft and beautiful as a swan gliding down a quiet river. But just wait a minute.

I am in a stone barn with a company of western Canadian machine gunners who are going to be in battle soon. . . . Plainly . . . in front of me, not half a mile away—is the powerful German strongpoint of Carpiquet village and Carpiquet airdrome, two or three miles west of Caen. That position has been a thorn in our side. We can't get Caen until we get Carpiquet. And now we're going to get it.

We can see Germans moving from time to time in the half light. We won't see them when the barrage begins. Little white rabbits and baby ducks are playing at my feet. They don't know that this barn will soon be shelled and machine-gunned. There's Carpiquet. There's the wood from which the Canadian regiments and tanks are going to attack. And here are we, closer to Carpiquet than to the wood. The attack will come across—right in front of us and toward us. I've never had a better observation post for a battle. And I dread what I'll see through this door.

Many hundreds of guns will support the assault. No less than hundreds of field guns—twenty-five pounders; no less than hundreds of medium guns, and many heavy guns; and in addition, sixteen-inch guns of a British battleship which will throw over two-thousand-pound shells from ten to twelve miles away at sea. And in addition to all that, many squadrons of fighter-bombers and rocket-firing Typhoons. This unimaginable barrage will move up, followed by our troops and tanks. I wonder if the Germans over there can guess that Hell is about to

break on their heads. At five o'clock—and it's now about ten seconds
to five. One — two — three — four — five — six — seven — eight — nine
— ten — eleven — twelve — thirteen — fourteen — fifteen — here she
goes.

And here, the sound having taken some extra seconds to
reach the microphone from the gun positions, the roar of the
barrage, or as much of it as the recording channel would admit,
came on to the disc. Halton took up the tale later, after the
barrage had lifted and the infantry had gone in:

Since I spoke the foregoing words at five o'clock this morning, I've
seen the most spectacular battle I've seen in many years of war reporting. Before five o'clock, at first light, we could see the hangars on
Carpiquet airdrome, and the village. For the next hour we saw hardly
anything. A few minutes after the barrage started, the objective below
us was covered by a dense cloud of smoke and cordite fumes. In the
following recording you will hear German and Canadian machine
guns, and the German shells that fell on us, and my attempt to describe
something of what I saw. Fortunately for you, the sounds as recorded
on a disc are quiet and tame compared to what they are when we hear
them. Even bursting shells that shook us and blasted us sound pretty
tame on a disc. Listen to this and then imagine it at least ten times as
loud.

Caen—the city that was to have been taken on D Day—was
the big British and Canadian objective. Four days after the
attack on Carpiquet—on July 8—Halton and Ouimet were reporting the opening of the attack on Caen.
"To observe this battle," Halton said,

I took up a position with a British assault company—Lancashire men—
from which I could see both British and Canadian troops attacking.
And so once more I saw our men go through wheatfields and orchards,
as steady as mechanical men, through hundreds of bursting mortar
shells and sweeping scythes of machine gun bullets. It was a cracking,
splitting world in which you'd have expected men to go mad rather
than to be able to attack. There was no preliminary barrage; but
hundreds of our field and medium guns and some of our ack-ack guns
—for air bursts—and navy gunfire [Matt had written "the sixteen-inch
guns of Rodney," but the field censor altered it] were used in close
support. During one short period several thousand of our shells were
exploding on enemy positions in a wood about six hundred yards away

from me and I think that was the most appalling sound I ever heard; occasionally a salvo of naval shells would strike there with a paroxysm of noise and flame. I can't say I saw all this, because the enemy was mortaring us pretty heavily and I was in a deep slit trench with a machine, recording the sounds.

The first British and Canadian troops got into Caen on the morning of July 9. On the following day, the men had much to broadcast about as they surveyed the ruined city and talked with its survivors.

"The people of Caen," Halton said,

welcomed us in the reeking shambles of their city today. . . . Amid their thousands of dead and wounded men, women and children, most of them the victims of our bombs and shelling, amid worse wreckage than I've seen in any war or campaign, amid fire and smoke and bursting shells and diving enemy aircraft, with street fighting a few hundred yards away, several thousand people of Caen came out of the ancient abbey church were they'd been taking shelter, to watch the flag of France broken from a masthead, and to sing the *Marseillaise* with strained and broken voices and with tears running down their cheeks. . . . We hadn't expected anything like this. On the night before D Day we poured down a thousand tons of bombs on Caen, and two or three nights ago we turned four hundred and fifty Lancasters loose on the town. In addition, we've poured hundreds of thousands of shells into it. We did expect to find some coolness if no actual hostility when we met the survivors of Caen. But this morning they welcomed us with open arms and with tears of joy.

I and my colleague Marcel Ouimet got into the town early this morning. The smoking shambles of the streets were still deserted except for our fighting men, and engineers clearing mines, and French Red Cross workers and police looking for wounded. At first the place looked like the end of the world, and I couldn't describe it if I wanted to. But working toward the heart of the town we found a few streets not totally destroyed. Then we came suddenly on a little square, the *Place du Lycée Malherbe*. There to our astonishment we saw a great church and school which weren't damaged at all.

The church was the famous *Abbaye-aux-Hommes*, a thousand years old. Two thousand people have been sheltering in that church for several weeks, and about four thousand more in the old lycée or school beside it. Not one bomb or shell touched the church. If you could go there and see the rest of Caen you'd say this was a miracle.

I went into the church and saw a tapestry of our times that I'll never forget. There were two thousand people in there, mostly women and children. They'd lived and slept and eaten there for several weeks. Babies had been born there at the foot of the sanctuary, and wounded people had been tended above the tomb of William the Conqueror, after being brought in from the shambles outside. Yet the great church was as clean and orderly as the halls of Buckingham Palace.

My colleague and I were almost the first men in British uniform these people had seen, though they'd known that British and Canadian soldiers got into the town yesterday. As we moved slowly down the great nave, hundreds gathered round us to shake our hands. All were calm and dignified, but their enthusiasm was deep and touching. And *they* thanked *us*. But they are the brave ones. When I was leaving the church a boy of seven or eight came up to my colleague Marcel Ouimet and said: "Are you going now to seek my father?"

"Where is your father?" Ouimet asked.

"In Germany," the boy replied.

On July 18 they were describing the opening of the British and Canadian drive south of Caen. With them in this battle was Arthur Holmes.

"This is the most savage push that the Allies have launched in France since D Day," Halton said.

It was supported this morning by the most colossal air attack of the war and one of the most intense artillery barrages in history. About two thousand, five hundred bombers dropped eight thousand tons of bombs. And at the same time and throughout the day, many hundreds of guns were throwing hundreds of thousands of shells. I have never seen anything like it. And, in fact, there has never been anything like it. A bombardment like that can't be wrapped up and brought home to you in words.

At dawn today we stood in our observation post on the west bank of the Orne River, looking at the loveliest morning we've had since we came to France. The air was soft, the dappled clouds were coloured in the most delicate pastel shade of pink against a pastel blue sky. The world was hushed as if it were waiting for the morning to break into music. But suddenly that world erupted under the greatest bombardment of all time.

First there was a far distant humming like the droning of a million bees. The first squadrons of the thousands of bombers were on the way. Soon we saw them, accompanied by hundreds of fighters, weaving and circling up and down the sky. The humming became an enormous drum-drumming, and the bombing became a roar that I can't describe. The German anti-aircraft guns began to bark and pop and crack. And ten thousand black palls of shellbursts appeared in the blue. And then came the bombing and then the shells. After the first few bombs we could see nothing across the Orne for smoke and dust. And in half an hour we ourselves were blanketed by smoke. We could only stand there feeling the shaking of the earth, hearing the long, long, continuous, monstrous splitting of the huge bombs, and the rolling, shattering drumfire of the guns.

That was a day for descriptive writing. Bill Herbert had come up to the front from his fighter station with Stewart MacPherson of the BBC and Don Fairbairn. Here is part of what he broadcast:

I watched this concentrated bombing this morning, and I am still shaking, so terrible were its results. It was a beautiful dawn. A few clouds rippled the sky, and the sun was a blazing circle in the east. The quiet before the attack was deathly. Looking down on the sleeping villages below, your thoughts were not of war but of peace and contentment. As the sun mounted, it shone on the wispy clouds, turning them to a shining gold, salmon pink and purple. At 5:37 we heard the distant whine of engines. The first aircraft were coming in. In three minutes the sky was obliterated. The earth shook, and the air was shattered with the loudest discordant symphony of bass drums I've ever heard. The attack had begun.

One of the first targets was a factory with two large chimneys, which the enemy had been using as observation posts. The factory and the chimneys dissolved as the first bomb load struck it. It collapsed in a pile of rubble. The bombs threw a red flash high into the air. The sky was laced with plumes of smoke as more bombers and still more bombers roared inexorably forward. I wrenched my eyes from the hypnotic spell of watching the bombs drench the area to look into the sky. As far as I could see, bombers filled the air. High above them, like eager shepherds, the fighter-bombers darted. The earth reeled with the noise. The ack-ack, by normal scales, was intense, but it seemed puny and insignificant against the relentless flood of four-engined planes.

At six o'clock this morning, night had fallen again, a night brought on by the columns of black and grey smoke and the dust churned up by the bombs. The clouds of dust billowed up to form a big V in the sky. By this time fires were raging everywhere, shooting shafts of grey and purple and black smoke thousands of feet into the air. Indeed, sometimes the bombers were obscured by the clouds. The smoke saddled Normandy like a thunder cloud. Ack-ack bursts pockmarked the sky. Twice I saw hits on our aircraft, and twice the black sky was slashed with a bursting smear of white burning aircarft, streaking like comets in a dizzy spiral to the ground.

Bill was lucky to make that broadcast. Just before the first planes came over, he and MacPherson and Fairbairn had been sitting on a low wall, chatting with two British soldiers in slit trenches. Mortar bombs began falling around them and they dived to the ground. When the mortaring was over, the two soldiers were dead.

All the reporting was not of battle, though. Bill Herbert offered a change of mood a few days later with some observations on the weather that had brought air operations to a standstill:

The rain is pelting down so hard that sometimes it's difficult to see more than a hundred yards. Visibility is completely on the deck. Living in a tent on a day like this is hell. Small rivers cascade down the flaps and into the water trenches dug around the bottom of the tent. Several times today I've seen these trenches filled to overflowing, and a deluge floods the bottom of the tent. There is a mad scramble to get personal things on to something solid, but it's no use. The water is endless and floods everything. The only thing to do is make the water trench deeper, so you grab a pick and shovel and start to work. The rain drenches you and your uniform, and rivulets run down the back of your neck. Everything you possess is a damp, soggy mess.

Eventually the trench is deep enough, so you go inside for a look around. The mud in your tent is ankle deep. Your bed, if you're lucky enough to have one, sinks lower and lower into the mud. You pile stuff on top of your blankets until the bed will hold no more. As you straighten up, your head hits the side of the tent and immediately it starts to leak. Water drips on to your blankets and you hurry to put them out of the way underneath all the other wet stuff. You give up in disgust and light a cigarette. Your hands are so wet that the cigarette paper comes off and you throw away the pulpy tobacco to the accompaniment of a resounding censorable cuss word.

By then you decide you'd better change your clothes as you balance precariously on the edge of the bed. Eventually you get some clean clothes on. You decide to take a walk and see how the fellows are getting on next door. Next door it's the same picture. They have a chair, so you sit down and laugh at their discomfort. You realize that you're not welcome, and shove off. Just as you're half-way to your tent you slip and fall and are immediately plastered with mud. Everybody comes out to have a look and to laugh uproariously. You drag yourself to your soaking tent and decide to go to bed.

As you lie in bed between blankets that are not so wet after all, you begin to chuckle and then you start laughing out loud. Just then somebody goes by whistling "I get the blues when it rains." You listen and you hear music from a radio. In the other direction some of the boys are singing, and from another tent, gales of laughter pour out. The rain makes soft music as you drift off to sleep.

Halton, Ouimet and Holmes had a grandstand view when the Canadians introduced one of the brilliant innovations of the war. The idea of moving infantry in armoured vehicles through the enemy's defensive fire on to its objective had been raised before at various times. It was Lt. General Guy Simonds, commanding the 2nd Canadian Corps, who developed it and first put it into practice, with complete success, in the attack that opened the drive to Falaise and marked the beginning of the German defeat in the West. To the surprise of carrying the infantrymen forward in bullet and splinter-proof vehicles, Simonds added the further surprise of attacking at night. He employed various ingenious means of guiding the attack on to its objective: radio beams; searchlights directed at a low angle along the axis of advance creating artificial moonlight by reflection off the clouds; and the tracer shells from Bofors guns, streaming over the heads of the attackers, to point the way.

General Simonds himself briefed the war correspondents beforehand on his plan—it had taken prodigies of co-ordination, and prodigies of labour to have the armoured carriers ready. More than twenty years later, Holmes was chatting with General Simonds at a reunion of war correspondents, and recalled the briefing.

"It seemed strange to us," Art said. "We'd looked on you as rather conservative, and it was so novel, and you were so confident."

The general laughed. "You didn't think I was a bit nervous?"

Holmes has special cause to remember the start of the attack, since for a moment it seemed to threaten his long bomb-proof record. He rode to his observation point in a jeep, one of a long column of vehicles on its way to the jump-off point. Coming up from the rear area, the vehicles had been allowed to use lights— the small amount of light that came through narrow slits in otherwise blacked-out headlights. But the Germans were nervous, and they had their air force up. There came the sound of aircraft engines, and simultaneously, over a loud hailer, the order to extinguish vehicle lights. The driver of the vehicle behind Art's—obviously one so newly-arrived that it had not had its headlights treated—pressed the wrong switch and turned his lights full on, throwing Holmes and his jeep into brilliant illumination. And looking up, Art saw a giant span of wings as a low-flying enemy bomber ghosted overhead across the road. The second or so that followed were long enough for Art to recall the whole Blitz, and to reflect that this, at last, might be it. But the driver behind got his lights out, and the bomber passed.

Halton left the description of the vehicle-borne infantry attack to an infantryman who had been in it:

"Five miles south of the line where we started from yesterday," he reported on August 8,

I met a Canadian soldier coming out of the battle with two prisoners. He told me something about the great fight yesterday. He was Private Thomas Fitzpatrick of Brantford, Ontario. A big, quiet young man who'd had extraordinary adventures.

"We were all excited," he said, "when we got into those big armoured troop carriers. We said it looked as if our generals had got brains. You see, the tough thing in battle is not to take the enemy positions once you get into them, but to get up to the enemy without the whole regiment being wiped out on the way across those fields. As soon as we saw those armoured carriers we knew someone had had a brain wave. We were going to get to the enemy without being killed by machine gun bullets on the way. And it was night, so the enemy shell fire couldn't be accurate, and the navigating was done for us by our own ack-ack guns firing tracer shells right over our heads. It was a terrific sight and pretty nerve-racking. We thought all those shells were coming right at us. All of a sudden, after only three-quarters of an hour, we were right in the enemy positions.

"We are full of excitement and hope," was Matt's opening for that broadcast.

General Crerar's First Canadian Army has broken through two powerful enemy defence lines south of Caen and is still maintaining its
momentum. There's still no swift rush southward. We're not yet in
Falaise. The German Army is not disintegrating. Not yet. In fact they're
still putting up a bitter fight for every village. They know, as we know,
that if we break through there, it's the beginning of the end of the
German army in the West. And slowly, we are breaking through. And
we all know that history is alive right here among us. Men press forward saying: "Perhaps this is the last great battle of the war."

Matt was not proof against an army's optimism, but optimism
never altered his sombre view of war or dulled his concern for
the fighting men.
    "Today," he said,

I visited a dozen British and Canadian brigades and battalions on that
packed, fast-moving and confused front south of Caen, and I've been
through some of the terrible little villages where the Canadians have
had such cruel fighting in the last three weeks. Places like May-sur-
Orne and Tilly-la-Campagne, where there were still odd German
snipers this morning. Words can hardly tell the difference between
these fields and villages south of Caen, and the Brittany front. There,
in Brittany, hardly a house is damaged. Here, south of Caen, hardly
a house is standing. Quite literally there are millions of shell holes and
many thousands of bomb craters. And all the wheat fields are now
churned up into fine powdered dust. Down there today, I felt I was
back on some desert battlefield. . . . It's really an appalling battlefield.

About that time, between the fighting for Caen and the drive
for Falaise, the CBC home office had the idea of utilizing some
of the great pool of talent in France by getting reports and com-
mentaries from correspondents other than its own. The execution
was entrusted to Halton, and he lined up talks by the English
correspondent and author Douglas Read and the Canadians
Ralph Allen, Ross Munro, Lionel Shapiro, Gregory Clark, Fred
Griffin and Gerald Clark. He also invited one from Charles
Lynch, but turned it down when Charlie showed him the script,
for it was all about Halton. Lynch thereupon went privately to
Paul Johnson and got his talk recorded, so it got to London and
thence on to the Canadian air anyway.
    Charlie began by saying: "I'd like to talk about my friend

Matt Halton," and after a few words about how they had met in
the days before the invasion, went on:

We were a strange pair—the most experienced war correspondent and
the greenest. It was just four months before that I had left my desk in
Toronto to come overseas as a war correspondent. Matt gave me my
first feel of the war as we talked about the war in Spain, the Finnish
war, the war in the desert, in Sicily and in Italy. He'd had his fill, and
I asked him why he was coming back for more. He couldn't tell me.
It was just one of those things. Probably it was because he had been
fighting the Nazis in print since 1933, and wanted to be in on the kill.
Actually, I think we were both there for the same reason. Here was
one of history's greatest military operations, and we were going on it.
     The next day was D Day, and Matt and I came in over the beaches
together. Matt went right to work, telling the magnificent story of the
Canadian fighting men. While many of us were writing about our own
personal experiences in that first hectic week, Matt was seeking out the
front line soldiers and telling their story in a way that I hardly ap-
preciated until I saw some of the grateful messages that came to him
from mothers back home. Sometimes I thought that his stuff was
flowery. Some of his scripts seemed that way when he showed them
to me before going on the air. But when the finished broadcast came
through you'd realize his artistry and his knack for catching in words
something of the thing called war.
     Matt's one of those fellows to whom you wouldn't talk about per-
sonal bravery. I don't think it ever occurs to him. He hears of a battle
so he goes to it. He's been doing that for almost eight years now. I
actually think he enjoys it. He comes back after a day in which he's
been under shellfire most of the time, and you ask him where he's
been, and his reply is: "Oh, I've just been up smelling the war."
     One of my hottest experiences in France has been to be pinned
down in an orchard for an hour and a half, while mortar shells were
bursting all around. I finally picked myself up and ran for the road,
and there grinning at me from behind a huge log was Matt Halton.
He had his portable recorder with him, and he said he'd just made
the best recordings ever made of a battlefield. It's a commentary on
the man that when we got back to find the machine hadn't been
working, and that his records had no sound on them, he didn't tear
his hair. He sat down, and he wrote one of the finest battle descriptions
that I've ever read.

     If there was little rest for the soldiers or airmen during the
push to Falaise, there was also little rest for the correspondents.

Their day would probably start with a briefing at army or corps headquarters. Then there would be a great piling into jeeps and a great scattering as they started on their day's rounds. There was always too much ground to cover, but everything was done by the military authorities to help. Canadian Army Public Relations, for instance, provided conducting officers, jeeps and drivers. General Eisenhower had said before the invasion that he regarded the war correspondents as "quasi staff officers," and they were treated accordingly. On getting to any headquarters or command post, they would be "put in the picture" as promptly as the exigencies of battle permitted.

August 14 found Halton reporting:

At noon today, under a glaring sun, the First Canadian Army launched another great attack in the direction of Falaise, supported by powerful waves of heavy and medium bombers. The high ground dominating Falaise is a roaring inferno as I speak. The enemy is fighting desperately. A master stroke has begun towards achieving the end of the German army. A few miles today means disaster for the German armies in the West. And every soldier knows it. Every soldier was shown the map.

On the same day, Bill Herbert broadcast:

The German is trying desperately to bring his motor transport out of the Falaise Gap. Canadian pilots of the 2nd Tactical Air Force, with whom I spent this afternoon at their dispersal, as they came and went from sorties, told me that the enemy has thrown caution to the winds and for the first time is moving his transport in force in the daytime. However, our aircraft roam the skies at will. There were no enemy fighter planes about today and there was little if any flak. The whole sector was alive with transport on the ground and our planes in the sky. There was complete and utter chaos on the road. The Germans were being forced to use the back lanes and the narrow winding country roads as well as the main highway from Falaise to Lisieux to try to release their transport. It was impossible, the pilots told me, to determine exactly who hit what and when, so great was the concentration of our aircraft in the sector. It seemed to them that the entire fighter strength of the 2nd Tactical Air Force, plus a few planes from the American sector, were out today, and the pilots were clamouring to their flight commanders for a chance to go out again and again on sorties. Fires were burning throughout the whole area. The woods were pouring up clouds of black smoke, and dust shot up into the air as high as one thousand feet in some cases. These woods were reported to contain concentrations of enemy mortars, guns, infantry and tanks. In ditches and in small fields alongside the roads, the pilots said that literally hundreds of vehicles—staff cars, armoured cars, motorcycles, small run-abouts, half tracks and other types of vehicles were blazing or smoking. Small units of infantry, caught on the roads, were strafed by our planes too.

The colossal disaster which had struck the Germans at Falaise was the prelude to the final liberation of France.

12–PARIS

The Battle of the Falaise Gap ended on August 21. Halton and Ouimet did not wait for the end. The Allied right wing was breaking out towards the Seine. The Americans were in Chartres, only 40 miles from Paris, and history beckoned. Lt. Col. R. S. Malone, the same Dick Malone whom Peter Stursberg had seen escorting a surrendered Italian general in Sicily, now in command of the Canadian P.R. group in North West Europe, had arranged with the Americans to allow a small party of Canadian correspondents to get in on the liberation of Paris. He discussed it first with the correspondents with agency priority. Ross Munro and Bill Stewart of The Canadian Press elected to stay with the Canadian story, but Halton and Ouimet decided that as the outcome of the battle was a foregone conclusion—our artillery was by then firing over open sights at the fleeing German transport—the big story was going to be the liberation of Paris. So they went, with Harold Wadsworth as their engineer. Speaking from Chartres a couple of days later, Halton said: "The day before yesterday I was with the Canadian Army. It had just captured Falaise. It was just breaking out from the fierce positions where the bulk of the German army had concentrated against us from the beginning. A Canadian brigadier said: 'You're not leaving us now?' And certainly it was hard to leave the Canadians even for a few days. But Paris was calling."

They went the long way round, by way of Saint-Lô and Cherbourg, around the Brittany Peninsula and through Rennes,

Laval and Mortain, the very recent scene of a great American victory, to Chartres, where they had to wait since Paris was not yet free. They got there on August 20, and were joined a day later by Holmes and Johnson, in the van, both lucky to have made it. Holmes had missed the turn-off for Chartres and was bowling merrily straight for Paris when he was waved to a stop by an American soldier.

"For God's sake don't go any farther," the soldier said. "You'll get mown down."

At that stage there had been no time to consider where the Canadian party would set up camp when it reached its journey's end. Now Malone, knowing that Ouimet had lived in Paris as a student before the war, took counsel of him, and Marcel had an inspiration. He suddenly remembered that the Scribe Hotel, ideally situated in the centre of Paris, close by the Opéra, was owned by the Canadian National Railways, and thus, as Canadian property, could be taken over without the fuss of requisitioning a building or the delay that that might entail. They conveyed the happy intelligence to Malone's opposite number with the Americans, and that was how the Scribe Hotel became the Allied press headquarters in Paris until the war ended.

Chartres was the first taste of the joy of liberation, for Caen had been overwhelming tragedy. Still there were dreadful enough things to see and hear in Chartres: the bodies of men and women murdered by the Nazis in their last days in the city, and many stories of other atrocities. They watched the funeral of some forty or fifty men of the resistance who had been caught by a German counter-attack, in a gap between Patton's racing tanks and the slower infantry, and killed to a man. Then the word came that they could get through to Paris, and they took to the road again. There was an overnight stop on the way—that was the night of August 24—because the road ahead was not yet fully cleared. But on the 25th, Halton was saying into a microphone somewhere on the road:

We strain our eyes through our field glasses, staring into the August haze for the first sight of Paris. We stare at villages and towns, we stare across one of the loveliest countrysides on earth. We stare for Paris. Paris is a symbol. Paris is victory. Paris is freedom. Paris is democracy. All the things we've fought for are in the word "Paris." And in Paris right now, people are fighting in the streets, and watching for us, as we advance hand in hand with history.

To put them in a simpler dimension, Halton and Ouimet were advancing side by side on the back seat of a jeep, mixed in with a tank column of the French 2nd Armoured Division and followed in the procession by Holmes and Johnson in the recording van. Johnson drove and Holmes took pictures, thus obtaining, as they entered the environs of Paris, a pictorial record of his colleagues literally disappearing under the embraces of enthusiastic Frenchmen and French women. It was like that all the way from the outskirts, through the Porte d'Orléans and into Paris proper. But the Canadian party had to make a halt when it approached the Seine and the Pont Neuf, for the bridge was being strafed by German machine guns and 88's; there were still German troops in Paris, though most of the garrison had left and the underground army of the Maquis, which had been fighting in the open for several days, had won control of much of the city. Having come so far to take part in a liberation, it would have been pointless to court death in an attempt to cross the Pont Neuf.

There ensued a lot of telephoning. A man in the crowd—he turned out to be a Canadian soldier of the First World War who had stayed in France—came up and spoke to Malone, and just happened to mention that the telephone system was still intact, the Germans having forgotten to cut the lines. Malone, Ouimet and Halton were out of their jeeps in a flash. From the nearest store, Malone called the Scribe, and found himself talking to Louis Regamey, who had been the C.N.R. agent-general in Paris until the occupation. Regamey told him that though there were German soldiers still fighting close by, the Scribe itself was a safe place if he could find a way of getting there. Halton thereupon called Information, asked for the headquarters of the Maquis, and to his amazement was immediately connected. He explained the party's need for a guide and was assured that help would come. Ouimet recollects putting in a call to the Scribe from the concierge's booth at one of the ministries. His account is the more detailed:

The female voice that answered said: "Hold on, Gentlemen, we'll be there in no time." In twenty minutes or so a black Citrôen drove up, and from it alighted an attractive young woman wearing a white blouse with a tri-colour armband and carrying a sub-machine gun. Her companions were two young men, also carrying sub-machine guns. She said: "You gentlemen get back into your jeep and follow us." And they led us through a maze of streets which they knew to be safe, across another bridge, and so eventually in safety to the Scribe.

Whichever one it was whose phone call had done the trick, it was Matt whom the attractive young woman, Christianne, flung her arms about and kissed, before she and her two male companions burst into tears. "Forgive us," she said. "We have waited so long. You are the first Allied officers we have seen."

Halton elected to ride in the Citrôen with the Maquis.

"We drove through the wildly cheering crowds with our arms round each other," he broadcast later. "We crossed the river to the Ile de la Cité, the cradle of Paris's history, and past Notre Dame, and then up the Avenue de l'Opéra to the Scribe Hotel. Here the crowds were just beginning to come into the streets, mad with happiness. And my friends were shouting: '*Il est Canadien*'—'He's a Canadian.' And I knew what it was to feel like a king. We were all kings that day."

Marcel modestly believes that the enthusiasm of the crowd for the Canadians was due to the fact that they wore the first British-style uniforms that had been seen in Paris since 1940. "And when they read on our shoulders the word 'Canadian,' it was quite a sensation. In fact, in no time at all a pretty fantastic party developed in the Scribe."

Ouimet was partly responsible for that himself. In his pre-war Paris days he had been acquainted with Louis Regamey, the man who had given the word that the Scribe was clear of Germans. They met in the lobby, and in the course of their greeting Regamey remarked that the Scribe's cellars were full of champagne which the Germans hadn't had time to carry away. Marcel's instant reply was: "Well, bring it up."

It was brought up and opened, case upon case. There was an interruption in mid-evening when Malone's signals sergeant, who had put up a radio transmitter on the hotel roof, made contact with the BBC in London and it was thus possible to send the first descriptions of the liberation of Paris to the outside world. Halton's and Ouimet's reports followed the usual route of relay from London, and those of the other three or four correspondents whom Malone was able to round up were sent by the BBC to their papers. At some stage of the evening, after they had rejoined the party in the lobby, Halton and Ouimet found themselves on one of the Scribe's small back balconies, responding to the demands of the crowd below for speeches. Ouimet recalls that they both talked about the fighting they had seen since D Day and, as impromptu spokesmen for the British and Canadian armies, conveyed regrets that these armies, being very busy elsewhere, could not be present at such a joyful time. On the following day Canada heard some exultant broadcasts in both its official languages, via the rooftop transmitter and the studio that had been set up in a room at the Scribe.

"Speaking from Paris!" Halton's voice came over the English network.

I am telling you about the liberation of Paris, about our entry into Paris yesterday, and I don't know how to do it. Though there was still fighting in the streets, Paris went absolutely mad. Paris and ourselves were in a delirium of happiness yesterday, and all last night, and today. Yesterday was the most glorious and splendid day I've ever seen.

We came in from the south. For hours we had strained our eyes for the first sight of Paris, and there suddenly it was, the most beautiful city in the world, and the people surging into the streets in millions. I don't know how we got along those streets. We were among the first vehicles, and the people just went mad. We drove for miles, saluting with both hands and shouting "Vive la France" till we lost our voices. Every time we stopped for a second, hundreds of girls pressed round the jeep to kiss us, and to inundate us with flowers.

The day of that broadcast was also the day of the shooting. At sixteen minutes past four, at the moment when General de Gaulle stepped out of his car to enter Notre Dame Cathedral, marksmen stationed on the roofs of buildings from the Arc de Triomphe to the Hôtel de Ville opposite the Ile de la Cité— Germans and men of Pétain's militia—began shooting into the crowds. Shots were fired at the general as he stepped from his car. As he walked up the nave of the cathedral, more shots came, from

Matthew Halton (right)
talks to German prisoners
in France

Gen. de Gaulle addressing a crowd in Chartres

The first allied flag flown in Paris is Canadian

Christianne of the French Resistance in Paris

Members of the French Resistance

V-1 in flight, but pursued

Wreckage of an unexploded V-1 in France

Execution platform, Breendonk Concentration Camp, with wreaths placed by Belgians after liberation

Road warning, Holland

The Scheldt—"The most appalling conditions"

Halton recording outside Aachen

Germans admit food for the starving Dutch

The link-up with the Russians on the Elbe

German officers surrendering to 4th Canadian Infantry Brigade

Blaskowitz surrenders to Gen. Foulkes in Holland

Stanley Maxted
aboard U.S.S.
Missouri in Tokyo
Bay on V-J Day,
with Col. Malone

behind the organ pipes and from the triforium. Remarkably, very few people among the thousands in the cathedral or the millions in the streets were killed.

The shooting nearly put an end to Matt Halton, Dick Malone and Christianne, the girl of the Maquis who had guided them into Paris. Malone wrote about it subsequently in his book. Having abandoned the attempt to get a car through the delirious crowd thronging down the Champs Elysées, they were on their way on foot towards the Place de la Concorde when the first shots came. With difficulty they got into a building that turned out to be the Ministry of Marine. Halfway up a great marble stairway bullets ripped through the windows at them, so that they had to fall on their stomachs and inch back down until they reached an alcove where they could flatten themselves against a wall while bullets flew past. It was half an hour before they could get out and back to the Scribe.

"Imagine for yourself," Halton broadcast,

four million people in a transport of happiness—and then three or four thousand mad dog murderers opening up on the crowds with machine guns, tommy guns and rifles. To have seen this is to have seen one of the foul things of all time. Who are the murderers? They were Germans and French fascists of La Milice. Mark that word, La Milice. They were French fascists who had joined hands with the Gestapo. Now, in their mad frenzy, knowing that the end of the world had arrived for them, they produced this frightful act of terrorism on the instruction of their German masters.

The shooting caught Holmes, Johnson and Wadsworth where it was heaviest—in the Place de la Concorde. It had been arranged that they were to wait with the recording van for their broadcasting colleagues at the Arc de Triomphe. When it became clear that Halton and Ouimet were elsewhere, the engineers joined the procession that General de Gaulle was leading down the Champs Elysées, Holmes taking snapshots along the way. They left it when it was time to get ahead to the Place de la Concorde and set up to record the speeches. The crowd from the procession was filling the Place de la Concorde when the bullets started flying. Holmes got out of the van and began taking pictures. He got one that showed men, women and children lying or crouching on a sidewalk. In the foreground was a woman half lying, half sitting, and laughing into the camera.

"She'd been lying down," Holmes explains, "and then she saw me standing there with the camera, and started laughing, and sat up. She must have thought it was funny."

Ouimet, as it turned out, had been in the parade down the Champs Elysées too, walking with some others of the war correspondents' party about fifteen paces behind General de Gaulle.

"I suppose I'll never see again so many hundreds of thousands of people gathered on one main artery of a city," he says. "The crowd estimate that afternoon was something like two to three million people."

Yet in that press he had an unexpected meeting, with a girl who had been a fellow student in Paris with him. "And to this day," he says, "this strikes me as an extraordinary happening. Who would expect to be recognized on the streets of Paris on a day like that?"

But the war was still on, and besides, the correspondents were under orders to leave Paris after three nights there so as to make room for another batch. As soon as the Battle of the Falaise Gap was over, the Canadians had been sent in pursuit of the retreating enemy. While Chartres and Paris rejoiced, they had been in bloody fighting for the Seine crossings and had then been directed to clear the Channel ports. So on the morning of August 27 Halton, Ouimet, Holmes, Wadsworth and Johnson said goodbye to Paris and headed back to the Canadian Army. The two broadcasters were still exuberant. Holmes got exasperated when they started reading aloud the cables of congratulation they had received for their Paris broadcasts. He had kept his engineering crew together with an iron hand amid the delights of liberation.

"All right, you two," he said, "Where were you when the shooting started in the Place de la Concorde."

It wasn't a talkative journey for the rest of the way back to the war.

On September 1, Halton, Ouimet and the engineers were with the 2nd Division when it made its triumphal return to Dieppe with scarcely a shot being fired in opposition, and the next day they made actuality broadcasts of the division's ceremonial parade, at which General Crerar took the salute. A week later they were reporting the liberation of Brussels by the British Second Army. These liberations were apt to be harder on a war correspondent's constitution than any privations at the front. At Brussels they found the celebration even wilder than in Paris. It went on for the best part of three weeks—though the first week was enough for them.

About the time of the Paris liberation, Stursberg and Lafleur also had a diversion from their routine duties with the troops in the line, this one afforded by the Allied invasion of southern France. Various military historians have dismissed this as one of the war's more needless operations, whose main effect was to rob the armies in Italy of their prospect of breaking through into Austria and striking the blow against the "soft under-belly of the Axis" that Churchill advocated. It took away much of their manpower and armament, and the landing craft they needed for planned amphibious operations. After the war Field Marshal Alexander, who had commanded the Allied armies in Italy, wrote:

Whatever the value the invasion of Southern France may have had as a contribution to operations in North-western Europe, its effect on the Italian campaign was disastrous. The Allied armies in full pursuit of a beaten enemy were called off from the chase, Kesselring [the German commander in Italy] was given a breathing space to reorganize his scattered forces and I was left with insufficient strength to break through the barrier of the Apennines.

It was an American and French operation. No Canadian troops were involved except the few in the First Special Service Force, though some Canadian ships took part in the preliminary bombardment and others carried troops. Stursberg had to go first to Naples and thence across Italy to Taranto, where he and an American correspondent were taken on board the United States destroyer *Hambleton*.

"Have you any liquor?" the captain asked after greeting them. Foreseeing what was to come, they reluctantly admitted the possession of a bottle of whiskey each.

"There's no drinking aboard this ship," the captain said, and they had to hand their bottles over. Nevertheless the captain, with fine courtesy, gave them his cabin and moved to his sea cabin.

The *Hambleton* was part of the bombardment group that was to cover the landing at St. Raphael. The day after Stursberg and his companion had gone on board, the group sailed, on a wide sweep south of Italy and then northward.

"It was an incredible five-day cruise," Stursberg recalls. "It must have been the last battle squadron that ever sailed. Our ship was part of a V-shaped screen of sixteen destroyers. In the V were two ancient United States battleships—the *Texas* and the *Arkansas*—and three cruisers, one French, one British and one American."

Stursberg got out his first report on the landings on August 16, and covered subsequent events until the end of the month. "Never before has so much territory been taken in such a short time in an amphibious operation," he reported on August 18. "More than five hundred square miles of beautiful sunny Provence are in our hands. . . . The Germans have already announced that we have entered Cannes."

In the ensuing days he watched the fighting that captured first Toulon and then Marseilles, and was taken by a Maquis escort beyond the Allied lines to the Vercors, the great plateau near Grenoble which had been the heart of the French Resistance. The invaders had liberated Avignon and reached the Rhone before he left.

Benoit Lafleur got there in less style than Stursberg, and it took him two tries. The first was with a US correspondent, in a light bomber. It was a long while before he would tell the story:

A sudden, unexpected storm hit us, violently shaking the plane nearly upside down, and we went into what I thought was an uncontrollable power dive. As we went down at great speed, we could hardly see the tips of the wings, and the ocean, as grey as the weather, was mounting towards us. The waves were ugly. In the cabin, my portable typewriter had hit the American correspondent on the nose, and his blood spurted out on the pocket of my battledress. "We've had it," he said, and strangely enough, trying to think of something, the reaction I had was to worry about what my office would say in Montreal. "What on earth was he doing there? Isn't he supposed to be with the Vingt-Deuxième in Italy?" At last, at about two or three hundred feet above the waves, the pilot managed to pull on the joy stick, so that he got us back to Bastia. We discovered that in the upheaval a raft in the fuselage had broken loose and made a hole in the tail. Had it been heavier, it would have torn the tail off the plane. The American correspondent wanted to write a story on the incident, and I begged him not to mention me, asking myself: "Is your journey really necessary?" as the wartime posters used to ask us.

Whether the journey was necessary or not, he made it, successfully at the second attempt, getting to Southern France and finding the armies already north of Besançon.

I was no more than a distant auditor to the broadcasts of the battles south of Caen, the entry into Paris and the excursions to southern France, having been summoned to Canada for discussions early in August. I thus also missed the last weeks of the V-1 bombardment, though with no great jubilation since I knew the rumours about an onslaught of rockets which was to follow the V-1's. Still it was nice, on getting back to London at the beginning of September, to be greeted by a hotel lift man with the words: "You'll have a quiet night. No more buzz-bombs." I was at the hotel because I had had to let the Harley Street flat go. With my co-tenants away at the war, it was too expensive.

13–HOPE DEFERRED

September 1944 began as a month of soaring hopes. The Canadians were capturing the Channel ports and the V-1 launching sites. The British Second Army entered Brussels on the 3rd and Antwerp on the 4th, and the reports were full of the scenes of liberation in Belgium. In Italy the 1st Canadian Corps had broken through the mountain defences of the Gothic Line and was poised with the rest of the Eighth Army for what army headquarters hoped would be a headlong pursuit across the Lombardy Plain and the last great battle. In London the Netherlands government, expecting the early liberation of Holland, announced that it was preparing to go home; the flying bombs had ceased, and the government promised the lifting of the blackout. In mid-month Halton and Ouimet were telling how the war had been carried on to German soil with the beginning of the siege of Aachen, and a few days later came the great news of the Allied airborne invasion of Holland and the plan to turn the enemy flank at Arnhem.

But the month ended differently. While we held Antwerp, it was to be November before we could use its desperately needed port. In Italy, the looked-for headlong pursuit had turned into another grinding advance against a new set of obstacles. In London, the Netherlands government had had to cancel its plans for a return home; the flying bombs had been succeeded by a new terror weapon, the V-2 rocket; the lifting of the blackout was minimal. And at Arnhem, the battle had ended in tragedy.

"I cannot tell you what liberation means," Halton exulted from

Brussels. "To know what it means, you would have to be in the Place de Brouckère right now. There are ten thousand people there. Many of them are dancing around British soldiers, and the rest are singing and dancing. . . . People who have been slaves for four years are wild with joy." From London, on September 6, Andrew Cowan relayed the news of the Netherlands government's preparations to go home, and I, that day, at the end of a broadcast on the cessation of the flying bombs and the promised lifting of the blackout, quoted the banner headline on a newspaper: "INVINCIBLE LONDON, YOUR BATTLE HAS BEEN WON." Cowan confirmed it a day later on the authority of the government. "The Battle of London is over," he said. "That's the welcome news Londoners got today from one of the men who know most about flying bombs—from Duncan Sandys. Except for a few more shots, we don't expect to see any more V-1's."

Yet in the early evening of the very next day, the still unaccustomed quiet was shattered by a mighty roar as the first V-2 struck London. It was a Saturday. The next day Cowan and I took a taxi to Chiswick to look at the damage after telephoning the Air Ministry and finding that that was where the "incident" had been. The descent of anything hostile, large or small, was always an "incident" in official parlance. Look was all we could do. The censors had been quick to forbid any broadcasting about it. The damage was relatively slight. The rocket had landed in a quiet street, in the middle of the roadway. The soft paving had let it bury itself deep enough to minimize its blast, so only the few houses nearest the point of impact had been badly knocked about. And it had killed only one person, all the other residents having been away.

The V-2 was a rocket and the forerunner of the whole breed of missiles which the atomic age was to produce. It was, by Second World War standards, an enormous and deadly engine, 46 feet long and five and a half feet in the beam, with a ton of high explosive in its warhead. It climbed and descended in an arc six miles high, and struck its target at a speed of two thousand miles per hour. That was approximately three times the speed of sound, so that the roar of its descent was heard only after the explosion on impact. Thus it was a silent menace from the sky.

The V-2's did not do as much damage as the V-1's, although

1,150 of them hit London and its vicinity, killing nearly three thousand people and injuring another sixty-five hundred. In some ways they were harder on the nerves. The immense roar of their explosion, the shock wave that could be felt a mile away, and the realization of their awful speed of descent, took some getting used to. You never knew one was coming until it had landed. The V-2 bombardment of London was to keep up almost to the end of the war. The last of them fell on March 27, 1945, only 39 days before the shooting stopped in western Europe.

Rockets or no, we had further portents of peace to broadcast from London in the earlier part of September. On the 12th, Cowan reported a meeting of the Labour parties from all the Dominions—the Canadian delegation headed by M. J. Coldwell— to discuss post-war policy. A day later he was on the air telling how for days past the London railway stations had been thronged with returning flying bomb evacuees, mothers and children in the thousands, coming home, although to the consternation of the authorities.

"They're returning," he said, "because victory's in the air and a government spokesman said last week that the flying bomb had been conquered. But they apparently didn't notice that he also spoke of the possibility of a last few shots. And that danger is still very real."

Across the Channel and the North Sea, the Canadian Army was stretched from Boulogne to Antwerp. It was a big story to cover, but in those crowded days Marcel Ouimet nevertheless found time for a flashback to D Day, by then a distant memory, in a reflective broadcast about his fellow French Canadians for the English Canadian audience.

June 6th—and on the sandy beach of the once charming but now badly battered village of Bernières-sur-Mer, a Canadian soldier lands. He's had to wade in, waist deep in the water, to lead the first column of the support company of his battalion to a dry spot. His battalion, the Régiment de la Chaudière, is the only French speaking unit on the assault. The battle has progressed favourably. The other companies are well in command already. A few shells and the odd bullet still are whistling by, but who cares? François has waited four years for this moment and his first words to a friend as he passes by are these: "C'est beau la France"—France is nice.

That day I was standing by the roadside when I heard those words, close to a group of wildly excited Frenchmen who had gathered about to see us come. They hadn't slept much. The bombing and the shelling had kept them all night long in their cellars or in their slit trenches. But now they wanted to greet the Canadians. The regimental patch on the Canadian soldier's shoulder soon attracted attention: *"Régiment de la Chaudière,"* one mumbled, and then he cried: *'Tu parles francais?"*—"you speak French?" *"Bien oui, je parle francais,"*—the reply came. "Yes, I speak French." *"Et tu viens d'où?"* "Where is your home?" *"A Québec."* With every word the Frenchman beamed. So he went on: *"Et quand serez-vous à Paris, la semaine prochaine?"* "And when will you be in Paris—next week?" The Canadian shrugged his shoulders and the reply came unexpectedly: *"Tet ben q'oui"* [*peut-être bien que oui*]—the French Canadian colloquial expression which comes literally, "well, perhaps yes," which like so many other colloquial expressions has been preserved among French speaking Canadians and which this soldier, a direct descendent of a family deprived for centuries of most of its links with France, had chosen to bring back three hundred years later to the land of his forefathers. On hearing it the Frenchman had grown more excited. "But you are not a Canadian," he said. "You're French—you're a Norman like me." And instantly he proceeded to hug the soldier and to kiss him on both cheeks. Now, in Canada most of the French Canadian families have done away with the well-known French tradition of the accolade—of the affectionate embrace between men of the same blood and race. So the soldier was somewhat taken aback. Nevertheless, he, on the sixth of June, had succeeded in capturing the heart and soul of France.

Today, like many more of his compatriots, he has been on this continent for over three months. He has lived beside the French, mingling with them whenever his duties allowed him to do so. He has been invited into countless homes, and his rediscovery of his former motherland has been most interesting to witness. *C'est beau la France!* A short and simple phrase of the French Canadian soldier on his landing at Bernières. Words which meant something to him then, but now they mean more. There is something concrete about them. The abstractness has gone. Yes, this country is quite a lot like he read in his history books: "That's my language they're speaking," he thinks. The village priest is still the inspiration, and the village church the centre of communal life. More since he began to rediscover France through Normandy, where the accents, customs and traditions, through their close association with those of French Canada, were the source of a series of striking impressions. Yes, some districts of Bayeux and Caen reminded him of his native towns: the tall church spires, the houses, the farms and their highly productive fields appealed to his imagination. He felt at home—much closer to home—and when he was forced to strike at other towns, somehow he felt badly. Something did tell him that in Normandy lay the foundations of his life and of his civilization. Why, on Sunday these people put on their best clothes and went to church. After Mass, they lingered in the square to exchange facts and ideas and inquire about the health of their respective families. These people liked to eat and to eat well, profusely. To eat a lot of bread, a lot of butter and a lot of cheese. But they didn't drink water. Instead they drank wine, cider and calvados—their native apple brandy. Rediscovery of wine caused a severe headache to many of our lads.

And what about the Frenchman's attitude to his cousin from Canada? One of great interest. He can't help being amazed by the peristence in the Canadians of a great number of French traits. He likes him. He sympathizes more readily with him than with his British and American allies, for the simple reason that he can understand him and knows he is understood. So he has opened his home. He likes to have Canadians for a meal or for a drink, to provide him with a family atmosphere and with some friends—3,000 miles away from Canada.

"C'est beau la France," say the soldiers of Quebec. But centuries of attachment to their soil and to their homes will bring them back no less deeply convinced Canadians, to a great and grand country, their native land.

Halton, ever since the June 6 landing, had been in mounting impatience for the day when the land war would be carried to German soil. So it was in a triumphant mood and voice that he broadcast on September 17:

This is Matthew Halton, *speaking now from Germany.* I am in a German forest with American troops. One of those dark German pine forests of legend which seem typical of so much in the German soul. I am in the command post of an American regiment just outside Aachen or Aix-la-Chapelle, and this regiment has burst the Siegfried Line. Occasionally there is the boom of guns, the sound which we've dreamt of for five long years. Guns roaring on German soil. And the wild echo in German forests. . . . It's still hard to believe that we're actually here, on the soil of the enemy, the holy soil, as he called it. Only thirty miles from Cologne and the Rhine.

He was there with Ouimet and Holmes. There was special significance for Halton in speaking from the vicinity of Aachen,

just inside the German border from Belgium. He had spoken of
the place in a broadcast only two days before:

Often, before the war, I sighed with relief when the train drew out of
Aachen and into Belgium and I was still free and could breathe again.
And I wonder how many hundreds of shaking refugees, trying to get
out of Germany, have been dragged off the train at Aachen and kicked
to the concentration camps. I saw pitiable scenes at that railway
station years ago, when few believed or realized that the most evil
thing in the history of Christendom had begun to snarl.

In the optimism which still prevailed in mid-September, Matt
had permitted himself, in that earlier broadcast, some specula-
tion about means of bringing the war to a speedy end. "Some of
us wonder," he said,

how the enemy will be able to hold out very long when the big Allied
attack is really mounted and delivered. The enemy has the great advantage the defender always has. It doesn't matter much. We're going to
crush him anyway. We have a brilliant and audacious General Staff;
none better in the history of war. No doubt the General Staff still has
something up its sleeve in the way of manoeuvre. The Rhine is a broad,
swift river, a terrific obstacle. You can't put Bailey bridges across the
Rhine. But perhaps there are ways and means.

He would not, after that reference to crossing the Rhine, have
been off to Aachen if he had known what was even then happening. The Canadian Army was not involved in the battle of
Arnhem, and since its planning was such a secret it is no wonder
if no advance word of it reached the Canadian correspondents.
But the operation did involve the Royal Canadian Air Force, and
Corporal Fairbairn got a tip-off from a friendly group captain.
Thus on the day that Halton and Ouimet and Holmes listened to
the sound of American gunfire in Germany, Don and his driver,
armed with a map reference and a time schedule, parked a recording van in a field near the Belgian-Dutch frontier and made
ready for what was to come. And when it came, he was saying
into the microphone:

That roar which you hear is from hundreds of our transport planes
passing overhead, carrying airborne troops to be dropped in an offensive against Germany. In this bunch above me now I have counted
roughly forty-nine. On all sides of these transport planes are fighters.
These—they are Lightnings at the moment—are whistling around,

protecting them. Now here come other fighters from another direction. They're sweeping in very low. The transport planes are not flying very high, so you must hear the sound of them. These fighters are coming in now from all directions. The sky is literally full of aircraft. They look just like bees forming around this batch of transport planes carrying the airborne troops. The fighters are still coming. Wherever I look, all the way around us here, are fighters. You probably can't hear them as well, because they're flying a little bit higher.

Two minutes have passed since that last lot of transport planes went over our heads, and now here comes another batch. Once more the fighters are approaching from various sides. These are Mustangs, Havocs, Lightnings—almost every kind of fighter which we know— whistling around the sky, protecting these aircraft as they go in to drop their precious cargo. Just where these troops will be dropped we cannot say, but they're on their way.

Fairbairn was back the next day:

"These troops are being dropped on the water lines in Holland," he said. He was not allowed to be more specific.

"From this point," he went on, "we can't quite see the troops dropped from these transport planes . . . we have been standing here now for approximately twenty minutes, watching these aircraft go over. Another lot is just approaching and, up until now, I can see that approximately three hundred have passed over our vantage point here." Later that day, back in Brussels, Fairbairn was at the microphone again, this time with an American airman. The circumstances were interesting. As he watched on the first day, two of the returning aircraft, crippled by anti-aircraft fire, had crashed close to his recording van. He had seen the crew of one of the planes bail out successfully, but only two parachutes came out before the second plane crashed.

"We hurried to the spot, picked them up and started out to find their plane," Don explained. "It was quite close to the German line, but after much bumping about fields and cart tracks, we reached it, and standing beside the charred wreckage were the other members of the crew. Beside me now is the pilot of that aircraft."

And he proceeded to interview Lieutenant Tommy Mills of the US Army Air Corps.

Hopes were high during the first few days. An airborne army

of three divisions, two American and one British, had seized the crossings of the Maas and the two branches of the Lower Rhine and the intervening waterways. If the farthest one, that at Arnhem on the northern branch of the Lower Rhine, could be held, the road to Germany was open and the end of the war in sight. To Halton the news was glorious.

"The airborne invasions and the lightning dash of the British Second Army," he said,

was one of the most brilliant strokes of the war. Probably the last big battle of the war in the West is now raging on the Holland Rhine. The battle for Arnhem is fierce, close and critical. The Germans are fighting desperately to prevent the junction of the oncoming Second Army and the airborne troops at Arnhem. Events of the greatest importance are happening in those few miles. History is watching two or three bridges in towns that most of us had never heard of before. . . .

He broadcast that on September 22. The battle came to its end—not the end that had been intended—three days later. The Second Army's guns, which might have tipped the scales, could not get close enough. Massive air support on the Caen and Falaise scale might have availed, but the weather had closed in and bombing was impossible. The survivors of the British 1st Airborne Division had to withdraw across the Lower Rhine. Halton recorded his *envoi* to the men of Arnhem on September 25, but censorship held it up until the 28th:

Today there is a glorious but tragic story to tell. The story of a gallant British division which went down to death in order to speed the defeat of Germany; the story of Arnhem in Holland; the story of the crossing of the Rhine; the story of the First British Airborne Division and of the men of the Second British Army. . . .

At first everything went well. The great armada of planes and gliders sailed over Holland and dropped the airborne divisions into bitter fighting at the key points on the three rivers. And as they landed, British troops sprang forward along the road. Look at what they were doing. They were stabbing forward in one long, thin line, into the heart of enemy country. There were a hundred and twenty thousand Germans on their left and the main German forces on their right. Yet Second Army troops rushed forward along that one road, because a great decision depended on boldness. General Montgomery knew it was risky, and he took the risk.

One American airborne force then dropped near Eindhoven to secure the crossing of the Maas, and the British troops linked up with them on the second day. An American officer said to me when I got to Eindhoven: "Whoever said the British were slow?" The other American force landed farther north at Nijmegen. The British got up to them after four days of fierce bloody battle along the road. Stormed at, counter-attacked from both sides of the road, throwing caution to the winds, they went forward and then, with the help of the Americans, got the Nijmegen bridge before the enemy could blow it. But the farthest away were the British airborne division. They had the toughest time. They had the landing farthest away from the Second Army, the landing at Arnhem, on the farther branch of the Rhine. They dropped from the skies right into the lap of the German SS troops. Right into one of the most fierce and dramatic battles of the war.

It went on for ten days. We watched, we hoped and we prayed. As Wellington at Waterloo prayed for night and Blucher, we prayed for good weather or for Second Army to get there in time. On the sixth day, advanced elements of the Second Army did get there and linked hands. But the weather failed us, as it has done so often since June 6th. Reinforcements came by air to the British Airborne at Arnhem—but not enough. We could not get enough supplies to them. We could not get enough men. More than once the reinforcements and supplies were flown in and then they had to go back because they couldn't get down. At the same time, the crack German troops, fighting with desperate vigour, and with superiority in numbers, kept attacking the thin finger of the road behind them—the obvious thing to do. There was Second Army rushing along that one road, both flanks exposed to powerful German forces. Three times the road was cut. For some forty-eight hours during those days the road was cut. And so, three or four days ago, it became clear that we were to lose the British First Airborne Division.

Four fifths of the great enterprise was a brilliant success. We are firmly established across the Maas and the Waal. We have a solid bastion half across Holland. But the last part is a failure—or rather, a brilliant but expensive success. Seven or eight thousand troops were dropped in the Arnhem area. About two thousand got away when the order came to get away if they could. About twelve hundred wounded were left behind. The rest—the other five thousand—are captured, missing or dead. When the war ends, let's remember those airborne men who died or were captured. The brilliant First Airborne Division is gone. Night falls on them. But the light of history falls upon them, and upon the graves of the men of the Second Army,

along the hard splendid road from the Escaut canal to the lower
Rhine.

The airborne landings and the drive of the British Second
Army were covered by some of the finest correspondents on the
western front. The great and intrepid Edward R. Murrow, veteran
of many a bombing mission over Germany, spoke into a microphone as his plane flew through the flak over one of the dropping
zones and the plane's complement of paratroopers stepped out
one by one and swung to earth. Murrow's CBS colleague, Bill
Downs, and the BBC's Chester Wilmot were on the ground with
the British Second Army. Charles Bruce, then London superintendent of The Canadian Press, flew on one of the desperately
dangerous supply missions to the Arnhem bridgehead. It was by
the skin of his teeth that he survived to achieve post-war distinction on the Canadian literary scene as poet and author. He was
posted as missing for some 36 hours. His aircraft, a Stirling
bomber with a Canadian crew, somehow got unscathed to the
dropping zone through what he afterwards described in a despatch as "a literal hell of flak," but was hit just as the aircraft
turned out of the zone. The plane went into a screaming dive,
and by the time the pilot had pulled it out, and the crew had
been distributed to trim the ship so that it would fly on an even
keel, it was too low for a parachute jump. Somehow they made
it to a belly landing on an airfield near Ghent.

The pilot sent a signal back to the RAF base at Fairford,
whence the mission had flown, but it somehow did not get
through. The next day Charlie got to Brussels and filed a despatch
for The Canadian Press, but it also somehow went astray. The
London papers published a brief report that he was missing, and
when he got back to his office it was to find his colleagues Ross
Munro and Alan Nickelson at work on his obituary, Munro already starting to type while Nickelson searched desk drawers for
material. I asked him around to the studios to do a broadcast on
his adventure. His account was laconic.

But Arnhem's highest reporting honours were won by Stanley
Maxted, who went in with the 1st Airborne and came out with
the surviving remnant. Maxted was not a member of the CBC
Overseas Unit but was a friend to everyone in it. He had been a

senior official in the CBC before he went to England and joined the BBC. Incidentally he was old for airborne operations, since he had been a captain in the Canadian Corps at Passchendaele in 1917. His call for the Arnhem job came suddenly. He wasn't told, of course, that it was Arnhem he was going to, merely that he had been given an airborne assignment, and was to travel light. He had just time to catch a train, taking with him only his portable typewriter, one of the small spring-wound recorders and a supply of discs, for an air base somewhere in England. Arrived there, there was little more than time for him to be fitted out with the camouflage jacket and the red beret of the Airborne before he boarded a glider full of troops and equipment. A fellow BBC correspondent went with him, though not in the same glider, Guy Byam, later lost in an air raid on Berlin.

There was no flying of recordings back from Arnhem. They had to wait for broadcast till the battle was over. But in the shelter of dugouts or battered buildings Maxted typed and recorded his reports day after day as the battle intensified and the perimeter shrank. Just before he came out at the end he smashed his typewriter and recording machine—the orders were to destroy all equipment—but he brought out, in the pockets of his jacket, a priceless record of the ten-day ordeal, in words and sound. These recordings were broadcast around the world by the BBC, but nothing was more dramatic than his account of how the remnant got out: by stealth, in darkness, through the enemy lines to the Rhine, across the river under fire, and then for the rest of the night trudging, soaked, mud-caked and exhausted, along the road south to Nijmegen.

The next two nights in London, the BBC Radio News Reel was wholly taken up with interviewing Maxted and broadcasting some of his precious recordings from the battle. The man who interviewed him was Byng Whitteker of the CBC, on loan to the BBC as a narrator for "Radio News Reel." On September 28th, Andrew Cowan went to the House of Commons, and came back to broadcast an account of Churchill's tribute to the men of Arnhem: "For those who mourn, there is the consolation that the sacrifice was not needlessly demanded or given without result. 'Not in vain' may be the pride of those who survived and the epitaph of those who fell."

14–THE SCHELDT

While the Battle of Arnhem raged there had been another story to tell. From Brussels, on September 20, Halton broadcast:

The Parliament of Belgium re-assembled today for the first time since May, 1940. This assembly marked an hour in the history of Belgium, and also in the history of free institutions. This was the first reconstitution of democracy in any country the Germans have overrun. There were moving scenes; there were tears and there was applause such as the chamber can seldom have seen since Belgium won her independence over a hundred years ago. When Prime Minister Perlot, who has led the Belgian government in exile for four years, ascended the tribune to speak, one felt that one was in the presence of destiny. There was a hush over the chamber. We were seeing the resurgence of liberty and the restoration of law.

Twice in a lifetime the brutal German has come clopping or clanking down the Belgian road. Twice in a lifetime the Belgians have been under the heel of an aggressor whose only law was the sword or the dive bomber. But now once more the people's man could ascend the tribune and speak. . . . The chamber was decorated with the flags of Belgium, Britain, the United States, Russia, France, Holland and Czechoslovakia. Any Briton would have been thrilled almost to tears in that assembly today, because the loudest cheers and the most prolonged applause were always for Great Britain and Winston Churchill.

We had another distinguished reporter at that occasion in Brussels—Pierre Dupuy, who went in his diplomatic capacity. On his return he broadcast:

131

The town was given up to rejoicing. Large crowds in the boulevards sang, cheered and danced. They were deliriously happy. Elderly people smiled behind their tears. They could not yet believe that they were free. The young people laughed trimphantly because they had escaped the clutches of the Gestapo. Brussels showed few evidences of the war. The British advance was so quick that the Germans had no time to destroy it. Only a few houses, occupied by the Gestapo, have been burned, in all probability to destroy their incriminating documents. This is why the Palais de Justice was burnt out. Here and there could be seen an abandoned motor car which had been stolen by the Germans in their rout. It was indeed a rout. It was described to me by Belgian friends who during three days and three nights saw the vanquished troops pass under their windows.

What a change since 1940. No more goose-stepping parades . . . and gone the arrogant young Nazis marching towards their conquest of the world. These troops were nothing more than a crowd of un- shaven, exhausted men, without arms and in ragged uniforms. Many of them were riding stolen bicycles, some without tires. Others were riding two and three together on farm horses or donkeys. Some of the ˉtaff cars, lacking petrol, were drawn by horses. Push carts and even baby cɔrriages were used for transporting the loot.

It is not difficult for you to imagine the feeling of our Belgian friends at the sight of this disorderly retreat. They dared not show their emotions while the enemy remained. Two young girls, who dared to laugh, were killed by a German officer. Immediately after the last of this lamentable cortège had passed, Belgian flags appeared. But it was still too soon. German armoured cars turned back again, to fire on the flags in impotent rage. Finally they disappeared in the distance forever. Brussels was free again after four years of physical and moral suffering bravely endured.

I stopped to talk to a brave Belgian of sixty years of age, who was standing outside a shop where the following notice had been put in the window: "Closed for Victory." He told me that the most terrible thing during the German occupation was the constant menace of the Gestapo. "We were like people condemned to death but who didn't know the date of their execution. One after another, people dis- appeared. Nearly every morning at about five o'clock I was awakened by the heavy boots of the SS on their way to arrest someone. Were they going to knock at my door? Oh M'sieu, you will never under- stand the joy that it will give me to be able to say: It is not the Gestapo, but only the milkman."

Two days after the re-assembly of the Belgian parliament, Halton reported a visit across the Dutch border:

In France the liberation was unforgettable. And it was unforgettable in Belgium. It was unforgettable to go into Germany. But it was also unforgettable, in a special way, to go with the victorious troops into Holland. When the stolid, phlegmatic, stubborn Dutch start dancing in the streets, that really means something. And we've seen them doing that. I drove into Holland this morning and visited the first large liberated town, Eindhoven. It's becoming a commonplace to go rushing across frontiers in your jeep, into one liberated country after another. My driver kept saying: "Are we in Holland yet?" And then, after crossing the Escaut Canal, and passing the graves of the British soldiers who had won the battle for that canal, we saw a girl with an orange skirt and an orange flower in her hair, and we knew we were in Holland.

But liberation brought tragedy to the graceful old town of Eindhoven last night. The Germans came back in bombers. Throughout the long years of occupation, Eindhoven had hardly ever heard the sound of an exploding bomb. But now, in the hour of freedom, hundreds of the people there were killed or wounded. Yesterday the town was *en fête*. Dutch and Allied flags flew from every window. Every woman in town wore the orange flower of the royal house in her hair. Hundreds of young women and girls wore orange skirts. Wine and refreshments were laid out on the main street for the British armoured forces and the American troops who had just linked hands. . . . And then the infuriated Germans came back. The Germans know that they are detested, and the knowledge enrages them. They are especially enraged because, even now, these strange people don't quite understand why they are detested. But a German officer said to me today: "We shall come back to these countries some day, and next time we shall really teach them a lesson they'll never forget. We'll teach them to put out their flags."

At the end of the month, the CBC team visited Breendonk, near Brussels, which until the liberation had been a Gestapo prison.

"I hate to tell atrocity stories, because I've been telling them for so long," Halton broadcast.

Much the same story that I now tell, I told ten years ago about concentration camps in Germany. But there are still people who ask if the cruelties of the Gestapo can be as bad as they say, and I think the concentration camp should be, in part, described. In this camp, several thousand Belgian and other resistants have been imprisoned at different times during the German occupation. Hundreds of them were tortured and killed in this camp. Before being shot or hanged, each man or woman had to build his or her own coffin. The bodies were taken to Brussels for cremation. Before the victims were murdered, their clothes were taken from them, and these clothes, many of them soaked with blood, were carefully ticketed and put away on shelves in a depot. And you can still see them there if you can bear to go in. Breendonk prison is an obscene place. But on the walls of the cells you can read an inspiring story of human greatness and courage. You can read the words that have been scratched on the walls by tortured and dying men. Things like this: *Long Live England; Speed the Victory....*

There in that place of evil memory, you wonder for a moment if there is any hope for a world which can produce such monstrosity. And then you see those scrawling inscriptions on the walls. Carved there by men and women (some of the names are those of women) after tortures too hideous to describe. And you know then that while there are devils in some men, there are gods in others. . . . That is a bit of the story of Breendonk. Part of the story of what we are fighting. And what we are fighting is not Germany alone. There are mad dogs in every country. The chief torturer at Breendonk was not a German. He was a Belgian fascist. The Belgian Resistance told me that the Belgian fascists were just as fiendish as their German masters of the Gestapo. The German military commandant of this area protested against the Breendonk tortures. So the point is that while there are mad dogs in every country, in Germany the mad dogs are in control.

The campaign on the Scheldt Estuary, in the western Netherlands just north of the Belgian border, was beginning for the Canadians. Its object was to clear the enemy from the banks, as far as the North Sea, so that Allied shipping could get into Antwerp.

"The story of the opening of the Scheldt," says the Canadian official history, "is long and unpleasant. It begins in mid-September. . . . It ends, so far as First Canadian Army is concerned, only on 8 November, when organized resistance ceased on Walcheren Island. There was much difficult, nasty and costly fighting in the interim." Field Marshal Montgomery took the same view in a letter to General Simonds, the acting Army Commander, near the end of the campaign. "The operations," he wrote, "were conducted under the most appalling conditions of ground—and water. . . . It has been a fine performance, and one that could have been carried out only by first class troops." Anyone who fought on the Scheldt, or reported the fighting, would heartily agree with both the official historian and the field marshal. Jack Scott, a young officer in Public Relations, destined for post-war renown in Canadian journalism, put the situation succinctly in a broadcast he made for us on October 18:

Our troops are continuing their push through a never-never land; part of it under water, all of it labelled with names that seem right out of the Wizard of Oz. If you're on the scene of these battles—and it's a sombre, bizarre scene in this godforsaken part of the world—it's almost impossible to realize that this is one of the crucial battles of the war. That the date of the final victory depends on the date of the victory here. For the battle is for Antwerp, thirty miles away as the plane flies. Until our troops have cleared the enemy from the flat, dyked fields on either side of the West Scheldt, Antwerp, the second greatest port in Europe and the answer to our supply problem, lies idle. Antwerp itself is a liberated city, almost unscarred by the war. The mighty cranes and docks and warehouses of its harbour are intact. But no Liberty ship with weapons, ammunition, food or gas will steam up the Scheldt until the Germans are beaten on its banks. There are said to be five thousand Germans in the pocket where the Canadians are now fighting south of the Scheldt, and they are resisting bitterly. Another eleven thousand are estimated to be on the flooded Walcheren Island and some four thousand on South Beveland, north of the waterway. These troops deny us the use of Antwerp, and so they're the number one priority for elimination. Every Canadian on that job knows it's important; knows that the final drive on Germany depends on the flood of supplies that will go directly through Antwerp. The enemy's stubborn defence is no surprise. And so the battle continues in the bleak, lonely marshes, and the Canadians are fighting for mud and water—and for one of the major victories of the war.

We had reason to be glad of Jack Scott's broadcasts from the Scheldt, because Halton wasn't there. Matt had been called home to make a speaking tour across Canada on behalf of the Victory Loan campaign. His absence made extra work for Ouimet. The

non-stop fighting demanded his presence with the front line units
every day, and he reported daily in English as well as French.
Every day meant driving out from Antwerp with his engineer,
Cliff Speer, through the most recent wreckage of the battle, between signs that said "Verges Unswept"—which meant that if you
veered on to the shoulder you were taking your chances with
mines—till they came to the final road block, or the forward command post, where they talked with a colonel or a major or with
corporals and privates. Here is a sample from a sample day:

Suddenly we came to a road block. There were no sights or sounds
of war, but five overturned carts lay on the pavement, and on one
of them was written: "The enemy is beyond this point." I looked at
our driver and at Cliff Speer. We decided to push some four or five
hundred yards further. The sign did not lie. We came to a crossroads where some of our tanks had stopped, and we hadn't been
there more than a minute before we heard the familiar whine of German mortars. They fell wide of their mark, but there was nothing
agreeable about them. At that crossroads the Germans had had bar-
ricades a few hours before. Trees that they had felled across the road
had been pushed aside, and some of our sappers were cutting them
up with their mechanical saws, while on both sides of the road others
were carefully picking mines out of the ground.

I walked over to Troopers Allan Gee of Nipawin, Saskatchewan,
and Edward Petrie of Edmonton and Thomas Patrick of Niagara
Falls [security allowed us to identify soldiers below the rank of
major]. "You had a hard fight?" I inquired. "Not too easy," they said.
"Yesterday Jerry was quite a nuisance with his shells. Every time one
dropped we couldn't see ahead for three or four minutes, and we did
have a close shave. At least a hundred and fifty pieces of shrapnel
hit our tank, but no-one was hurt." And with that they were showing
Speer and myself some of the dents on their tank. A little later we
got to the regimental headquarters. It was noontime, and there a few
hundred yards away from the fluid front, while mortars and shells were
whist'ing over our heads, we had lunch with the colonel and his
officers. The sounds of war did not even make a pause in our conversation.

The colonel was speaking. "The Germans," he said, "sort of react
violently once in a while. They're disorganized all right, but they
still put up resistance. Yesterday, for instance, they dropped three or
four hundred rounds in our lines."

"But this doesn't seem like very good tank country," I interrupted. "It makes one think of the Norman bocage."

"Tank country?" The colonel smiled. "I don't believe in this idea of tank country. In my opinion you can use tanks anywhere, provided you have artillery and infantry support."

A bell rang—the telephone. A nearby headquarters wanted the regiment to know that planes would be over in thirty minutes to engage some targets in the area—two German seventy-fives that had caused a certain amount of trouble. The adjutant took the message, and he in turn rang the squadrons: "Hello Baker, Easy, George and Roger. Hello Baker, Easy, George and Roger. Our air force is going to attack targets in the area. Be prepared. Have your recognition signals on hand."

It was twelve-thirty. At ten to one, with some of the officers, we found ourselves on top of the water tower. A thousand yards away there was another water tower. A major commented: "I wouldn't be surprised if Jerry were looking at us." Fifteen hundred yards ahead there was a wood, and a mile or so behind it, a church tower. The major said: "The wood—that's where the bombs are going," and then we heard the roar of ten Spitfires and four Typhoons. We were so close that we could see the bombs leaving the planes and falling madly to the ground. . . . We took our leave of the colonel and we drove towards Antwerp. We got to the barricade, which the colonel said had kept many a Canadian from running right into the enemy lines.

A day with another forward unit (we weren't allowed to identify units either, so he simply called it "a famous Montreal battalion") started well forward, at a company headquarters, and Ouimet began his report with the story of the company's latest action as told him by the company sergeant-major:

The attack was mounted at six in the morning. I don't believe I ever saw, or ever will see, heavier machine gun, mortar or shell fire. We had to cover three hundred yards of wide open ground. There wasn't a slit trench, not even a ditch, for cover, but we got to our objective and held it till relief came, in spite of the 88's and mortars, and in spite of the fact that the enemy was well-sheltered in brick-lined slit trenches with concrete and cement tops.

The second-in-command of the unit told him of their recent fighting: "Pushing over those dykes is no fun at all. The trouble is, with all the flooded areas, we can't advance in the field. We have to follow the dykes and the highways, and Jerry is quite clever at pinpointing the crossroads and the roads themselves. It's grim fighting."

"But the morale of the men couldn't be any higher—even though their life has been one of misery," the colonel interrupted.

Another officer gave Marcel a description of the "life of misery."

"My men have been living in their slit trenches for days," he said. "They're soaking wet. The trenches have been dug in super-saturated soil. And the level of the flood keeps rising. In a barn that we've been using as a sort of rest centre, where the boys could stretch out and sleep in the hay, the water's now completely covered the floor, and they've had to take to the loft."

Marcel spent a lot of that day with the other ranks.

"Leave?" he said at the end of his broadcast.

These Canadian soldiers have practically forgotten what one does on leave. They've been in the line continuously for weeks. They haven't seen Paris. They haven't seen Brussels, and they had only a few hours in Antwerp. But they don't mind hearing about the pleasanter aspects of life in those large centres. "We've got a job to do," they keep on repeating. "We're doing it as well and as fast as we can. If it helps to shorten the war, we'll be satisfied. And then we'll see Paris."

It fitted in very well that after the Scheldt had been won, Andrew Cowan was in Paris to broadcast about the handsome leave centre where Canadian soldiers, after mud-caked months, could glory in hot baths while volunteer helpers cleaned and pressed their uniforms.

I managed to get out of the office and to the front for the last weeks of the campaign. By that time the 3rd Canadian Division, pushing towards the coast along the south bank, were clearing the seaward end of the estuary, and the 2nd Division was beginning a new phase of the battle along the north bank. It meant traversing a narrow and stubbornly defended isthmus between the mainland and the peninsula of South Beveland, and then pushing through South Beveland towards Walcheren, the fortress island at the mouth of the estuary whose heavy guns kept the Scheldt sealed to Allied ships. There were some famous correspondents on the Scheldt, British as well as Canadian, for many British army formations were under Canadian command. Among the Canadians were Ross Munro, who had been in every Canadian army operation from the beginning, starting with the Spitzbergen raid; Ralph Allen and Lionel Shapiro, veterans like Munro and Marcel Ouimet of the Italian campaign and the D Day landings in Normandy; and Stanley Maxted, back to the wars from Arnhem. I had a fleeting glimpse of the fall of mortars that nearly killed most of them.

It happened in the South Beveland landing, an amphibious operation—"a capsule D Day," Ross Munro called it in the mess next morning—which ferried the British 52nd Division the five miles or so across the estuary from the south bank in support of the 2nd Canadian Division. Ouimet and I had the good luck to be in—and out—early that day, thanks to the enterprise and connections of Athol Stewart, who went with us as conducting officer. Athol knew some of the people in charge of embarkation, and thus got us waterborne while the rest of the correspondents had to wait through a long delay in the officially laid-on arrangements.

It was an interesting morning, from the moment when we lumbered through a cut in the great sea dyke and splashed into the estuary while much of the population of Terneuzen waved to us from the dyke top as if we were so many Sir Francis Drakes. We were part of a long procession of Buffaloes, strange amphibious craft that looked like tanks with the tops cut off and had tractor treads which were also scoops for propulsion through the water, so that each Buffalo threw up twin fountains astern. Things were noisy on South Beveland when we landed. The Germans were laying down a barrage on the estuary in front of the landing beach, I suppose from the big guns on Walcheren, for when the shells hit the water they sent up immense geyers. When we had got across the dyke and on to the flat, there was some rather haphazard mortaring, harmless enough in the empty fields it was hitting. But by the time we had made our rounds, including the de rigeur call on the brigadier to be "put in the picture", and were back on the beach, a change was apparent. The haphazard mortaring had got itself organized into a creeping barrage, and it was creeping towards the beach. While the ominous noise came nearer and Marcel explained that this sort of thing was liable to happen when the enemy got over his surprise, the idea of being waterborne again grew more and more appealing.

After what seemed a long time, Athol, who had been strolling along the water's edge with an air of utmost unconcern, found a Buffalo that was on the point of leaving, and we clambered on board. For the first few minutes we had no thoughts to spare for the mortaring behind us, our attention being fixed on the shell splashes in front. But our craft having got around them, there was an instant to look back before a sudden alteration of course hid the beach from view. And in that instant we saw fountains of sand go up as the mortars hit. It was a sobering sight, and although we all three saw it, nobody said a word about it, or about anything else, till we were ashore again at Terneuzen and back in the waiting jeep. What we didn't know, and wouldn't until Munro, Allen, Shapiro and the rest got back to camp late that night, was that the moment the mortars hit the beach was also the moment they landed. They did the only thing there was to do—fall flat and dig in with spoons, cups or whatever other implement came first to hand as they reached into their mess kits. They had to stay dug in for what seemed like hours, until the mortars were silenced.

Covering the Scheldt campaign meant a lot of long rides in the jeep. Two days after the South Beveland landing, Marcel and I were miles away at Bergen-op-Zoom, in the territory of the Canadian 4th Armored Division, which was fighting northward towards the River Maas, and in so doing, protecting the troops on South Beveland from the danger of attack from the rear. Bergen-op-Zoom had been taken the afternoon before we got there, but the Germans were still holding positions just north of the town. It would have been difficult for anyone to set up a headquarters closer to the enemy than the hotel room where we called on the victorious brigadier. The room overlooked a canal, and there were Germans dug in along the canal's far bank. So while we tried to ask questions and the brigadier and two lieutenant colonels tried to answer, the panelled walls quaked, the pictures on them danced and the air was full of thunder from the bursting of the shells which the artillery was lobbing over our heads on to the enemy positions. It was a most difficult essay at conversation until the brigadier telephoned through to the gunners and asked them to raise their fire a little before they blew brigade headquarters up.

The capture of Bergen-op-Zoom, like the landing on South Beveland, was one of the campaign's bigger battles, but before them we had had plentiful experience of what General Crerar, when he met some of us at the end of the campaign, called the "two-man front." By that he meant a front that often consisted of two lines in single file, one on either side of a dyke-top road. That was the kind of front it was on the day, at the beginning of the drive across South Beveland, when Marcel and I, with Athol Stewart and our driver, found ourselves with the forward platoon of the whole 2nd Division. We did it simply by driving through thinning traffic until our jeep was the only vehicle on the road and a certain stillness over the landscape warned us that it might be a good idea not to go any farther. A shell passed low over our heads, to prove the rightness of the idea, as we came to a stop on the first convenient bit of grass verge, and I, being new to the game, could only admire the act of levitation by which my three companions seemed to be up, out of the jeep and flat on the ground in the same instant. We crossed the road to look for cover, and from the foot of the dyke a very muddy lieutenant hailed us with the urgent advice to get down off the skyline and join him. We obeyed with alacrity, and at his behest sat with our legs in a slit trench for the greater ease of slipping all the way into it. It was one of a small system of slit trenches which the lieutenant and the men of his platoon had captured in a fierce little battle a few hours earlier. The platoon had been on the go without sleep for forty-eight hours, and everybody was dog-tired, but they told us their story with some zest, pointed out the next enemy position, two or three fields away, and seemed glad to see us. I think though that they were also glad when we went, after the shooting had stopped. Our arrival had excited the German gunners to a cannonade with their 88's, which brought on some counterbattery fire from our 25-pounders, and the business robbed them of the peace and quiet they were entitled to while they waited to be relieved.

One day near the end of the campaign word came to the press camp that the ancient town of Sluis, only a mile or two from the coast and part of the last pocket of resistance on the south bank, either had fallen or was about to fall. The long drive was not in vain, for there was plenty to see and hear when we had got as far as we could go, but the last pocket was still resisting with a great deal of noise, and the Germans in Sluis were putting up a brave last stand. We had troops right outside the town, but Marcel and I didn't get to see them because there were enemy snipers in the fields on both sides of the last mile or so of road. Somebody told us that Ross Munro had been down the road and back a little earlier, but we weren't moved to emulation. An appreciative tank regiment had made Ross the present of an armoured car, and he was using it that morning.

One battle of those days on which we never tried to get forward of brigade headquarters was the grim last act of the Canadian sweep across South Beveland—the assault on the causeway. It was a deadly business. Three quarters of a mile long, forty yards wide, and, in the words of the official history, straight as a gun barrel, the causeway was the link between South Beveland and the island of Walcheren. The retreating Germans had left it so thoroughly cratered that no vehicle could get across it. At the Walcheren end, behind a massive road block, there were artillery and machine guns with a clear field of fire down the causeway's length. How any infantrymen managed to get across seems a miracle now as it did then, but a handful did, though it took days, and held a tiny bridgehead on the Walcheren side until they were relieved by British soldiers of the 52nd Division.

The Scheldt campaign came to an end with the reduction of Walcheren, a task that took eight days from the first touchdown to the last shots. The battle began on the morning of November 1 with two landings, one at Flushing by means of an assault across the mouth of the estuary, and the other at West Rapelle on the island's west coast in an assault from the sea. Ouimet and I were at Flushing on the first day, though for some reason we went separately this time.

It was hours after the early morning assault when my landing craft crossed, but an enormous barrage was still howling overhead and the coast behind us was still alight with gun flashes as a great concentration of artillery poured shells on the German gun positions along the Walcheren coast. When we reached

Flushing we had to wait half an hour before we could land, and content ourselves with the spectacle of half a dozen Typhoons methodically rocketting a concrete strong point a few hundred yards away, because a German soldier concealed somewhere near was spraying the beach with machine gun fire. A lot of enemy marksmen had stayed behind, or else infiltrated back, to snipe from eyries high in the cranes and gantries around the harbour, and they, and the noise of the shells criss-crossing overhead, made for an interesting day. It was probably a fair sample of what was to go on for the next week until the last gun and the last prisoner had been taken. I suppose my most unforgettable memory of the day is of the debonair young major who came striding across a field swinging a cane and wearing a beret that made me feel over-dressed in my steel helmet. He invited me to go with him on a tour of the perimeter in an hour's time. I accepted, but wasn't altogether sorry when the sudden heavy shelling of a command post—it had recently been an enemy strong point—drove me and some soldiers I was talking to into the security of the post's concrete depths as the appointed hour approached. The young major was obviously the kind of man who bore a charmed life, but I had no such assurance about myself.

With Walcheren captured, 1st Canadian Army was taken off the Scheldt to rest and regroup, the advanced press camp, now at Breda, was closed, and Marcel Ouimet left for an overdue leave at home in Montreal. He got there safely, but only after a narrow escape from a V-2. He had to put in a few days in London on the way, and was using my flat. He had just got inside the front door one evening when the V-2 went off very close, the blast knocking him to his knees and showering him with glass from shattered windows. Five minutes before, as he walked along Wigmore Street from the office, he had paused at the side street which led to a pub across from Selfridge's, thinking to go in for a beer. Then on a sudden change of mind he had continued homeward instead. And it was on that pub that the rocket fell.

Antwerp had suffered a plague of V-2's throughout the Scheldt campaign, and they had been the correspondents' greatest trial until the advanced press camp was moved to Breda in Holland so as to be nearer the front. The Germans, incensed at having had to clear out of Antwerp without time to wreck the harbour installations, were trying to make up for the omission with rockets, and the press camp, in a suburb near the harbour, was constantly under fire. The camp was a large mansion or small chateau, and the glass of its windows had long since succumbed to blast and been replaced by boards, essential to the blackout. The bombardment went on around the clock, but the real nastiness was reserved for the nights and would be mounting to a crescendo by bedtime. I remember the mutter of protest that came, in the midst of a series of soul-shaking explosions, from a camp bed somewhere in the crowded attic where a dozen or so of us were trying to sleep: "This shouldn't happen to a dog." It was a difficult art to get to sleep instead of waiting for the next explosion, and the next. Probably the healthy outdoor life of the days was a help. By morning, invariably, the blackout boards put up the day before had all been blown in and daylight was streaming through the empty window frames. A V-2 chose an appropriate moment for a daylight landing close to the Army Headquarters building where the morning briefings were held. On this morning it was a special briefing, given by General Simonds himself. It was brisk and concise. Having made short work of the battle situation, the general asked—"Any questions?"

There were no questions. The regular briefing officer, who was almost as notably brisk as General Simonds, said: "Well, that's that," and on his second "that" a V-2 went off like the crack of doom. There was a wave of laughter, not untinctured with nervousness, from all over the room. The general, who had given no sign of having heard anything, permitted himself the shadow of a smile, and there was a grateful exodus of correspondents to jeeps and anywhere that wasn't Antwerp.

15 – THE DREARY WINTER

With the regrouping, the advanced press camp moved to a small village called Wijchen, a few miles south of Nijmegen. "A muddy, cold and crowded little camp," Halton, a connoisseur, was to call it on his return from Canada. Still, it had its advantages. Corps, divisional and brigade headquarters, and much of the front, were within easy reach. From Nijmegen you had only to go a few miles due east to reach the lines of the Canadian 3rd Division along the northeast tip of the Nijmegen Salient, or a few miles southeast to be with the units of the 2nd Division facing the Reichswald. Or you could go north, across the great bridge over the Waal, the main branch of the lower Rhine, on to the "island" between the Waal and the Lek and along the road that led towards Arnhem, until you reached the road barrier that marked the end of our territory and the beginning of the enemy's. You didn't have to go far to find a place where only the breadth of a small river, or a few fields, separated our forward positions from the enemy's.

The front was static, and this, as the official history points out, was fortunate, since the Battle of the Scheldt had left the First Canadian Army, and its three Canadian divisions in particular, thoroughly exhausted. The static period, the Canadians' only period of even relative inactivity in the whole campaign in North-West Europe, lasted exactly three months, from the end of enemy resistance on Walcheren on November 8 to the opening of the Battle of the Rhineland on the following February 8.

145

A static front did not mean an inactive one, however. There was constant patrolling, there were a lot of skirmishes and some small battles, and there were the enemy's constant attempts to destroy the Nijmegen bridge, the great prize of the Battle of Arnhem. And it was a vastly important front. Westward to the coast, the line of the Maas had to be held against the Germans in northern Holland; and the Nijmegen Salient was the potential launching area for eventual attack either to the east or to the north.

"The Nijmegen bridgehead," General Simonds wrote in a directive on November 6, "is the most important bit of ground along the front of 21 Army Group. Here we hold the only bridge across the main course of the Rhine. If the Germans accept a decision west of the Rhine, the eastern face of the Nijmegen bridgehead between the Meuse and the Rhine forms a base through which an attack can be launched against the northern flank of the German battle line."

That was how it turned out, and it was from just south of Nijmegen that Matthew Halton and Benoit Lafleur, on February 8, 1945, watched the opening of the Battle of the Rhineland. In the meantime, there was enough to talk about. It was still wet and miserable. The landscape around Nijmegen was almost as aqueous as that of the Scheldt. But the static nature of things gave time for visiting and for discovering, among other things, the talent of the Canadian soldier for making himself comfortable and cheerful in the midst of a howling wilderness. After the constant movement on the Scheldt, it was pleasant to be able to do a broadcast now and again on that line and be able to talk about well-built dugouts and the warmth that came from a stove made out of a steel ammunition box.

Benoit Lafleur had come in as Ouimet's replacement when we had been a few days at Wijchen. Benny, witty, quiet and charming, nevertheless struck alarm on his first day there into Bill Williamson, our tough and battle-experienced driver, who had been with Halton and Ouimet since early days in Italy. He went out in the jeep with Bill for a look around. They came first to the Nijmegen bridge, which German 88's were giving one of their periodic shellings.

"So I asked him where else he'd like to go, and he said 'We'll go across,'" Bill related to me that evening. "And when we'd got across, I asked where to now, and he said 'Let's go back,' so we came back, and the Germans still shelling."

"Why did you do it?" I said.

"I'll go anywhere an officer asks me," said Bill. Lafleur and I weren't officers, but that was beside the point.

Bill took his revenge not on Benny but on me, when a few days later he drove me into Nijmegen for a call on a colonel of Royal Canadian Engineers. The Germans were putting on a shelling, and the townspeople were all indoors although it was a Saturday afternoon. The shelling thickened as we cruised slowly up one street and down another, looking for the tactical signs which were supposed to guide us to the colonel's headquarters. We never did find the place that day, but as we searched, my enthusiasm waned, for the peculiarly nasty whistle that announced each shell grew shorter and shorter. Bill resisted my suggestions that we should get the hell out of there—I could no more than suggest, for I felt that his philosophy of where he was willing to go ought to cut both ways—and instead took a gruesome pleasure in explaining, unnecessarily, what the shortening of the whistles meant. But he got tired of the game at last and had started to speed up when he had to stop at an intersection. Just then a shell burst, with no preliminary whistle at all but a lot of smoke, in a front garden just across the narrow road we had come to. The shells had been coming in pairs, a second or two apart. We tore across, hoping to beat the second, which somehow never came. We got clear of Nijmegen, and Bill said:

"It's a good thing I always stop at intersections. Do you know what would have happened to us if I hadn't, Mr. Powley?"

"Yes, Bill," I said, raspingly, I hoped, "I know."

"I'm going to tell you anyway," he said. "We'd 've both had an assful of eighty-eight." We headed for the front, in the hope that it would be quieter than Nijmegen, and Bill got reminiscent. "That was the closest call I've had in the war, but for one," he said. "That was in Italy, with Mr. Ouimet." I wondered what Marcel had ever done to him.

The business I had wanted to see the colonel of Engineers about was the Nijmegen bridge defences. He was the man who had devised the ingenious boom arrangement, an adaptation of

Canadian logging practice, which guarded the precious bridge from the mines and the frogmen with explosive charges that the Germans had been sending down the river to blow it up. He arranged things easily when I did see him, and a day or two later a small party, which included John Clare of the Toronto *Star* and John Redfern of the London *Daily Express*, set out in a river tug for a close-up view of the boom. Our escorting officers were a major of Royal Engineers who began the voyage by running the burgee of his father's yacht club up the mast, and an RE lieutenant who was also a Yorkshireman and a giant. The sappers were doing maintenance on the boom that morning. Across the breadth of the river, as the gate opened to let us upstream, they were sprawled flat on the boom, drenched with spray and holding on hard against the waves that the turbulent current made. It was slow going upstream against the current, but we got as far as the bend that had to be the limit of the voyage because there were German gunners on the other side of it. We turned, and came sweeping down with the current. The idea was to put the engines hard astern as we approached the boom, but the civilian skipper was old, got confused and rang "full ahead" instead. The sappers, seeing us bearing down, clung on desperately.

"Aang on, laads," the Yorkshire lieutenant roared in a voice that the Germans around the bend must have heard, and we hit the boom with a great crash. They did manage to hang on. But it was one of those horrible moments, and we were a shaken lot when we landed. When we could laugh about it, John Clare said he'd never forget the look of frozen horror on the faces of the sappers as we came tearing at them.

Halton came back on December 16. His speaking tour of Canada—his broadcasts had made him a national figure—had been a tremendous success, but his elation was tempered. He had received much acclaim, which embarrassed him because he felt it belonged not to him but to the men he spoke about. During a few days' stopover in London he had sent a letter to Dan McArthur, one of his recent hosts.

"London is London," he wrote,

and that is all I ask of any town. I smell the fog as I emerge from dirty old Euston station, and I think: "I'm home." There are a few lights on the streets now; there are a few more craters and wrecked buildings . . . everybody here is excited and gloomy about Greece. . . . Everything is getting so complicated and difficult. It looks as if the war is only laying open, rather than healing up, the deep political and economic maladjustments of the times. Maybe the world isn't going to have a very fine time from now on. And I don't think most people realize how really serious the situation has become as a result of rockets and flying bombs and all the other Wellsian or Popular Science Magazine things that are actually coming to pass.

Strangely enough, Matt had to get to the Nijmegen Salient to make his first acquaintance with these Wellsian weapons; he watched a V-1 passing overhead and saw the trails of V-2 rockets rising into the sky from their Dutch launching sites. He had been in France through the V-1 bombardment of London, and had left the front before the V-2 barrage on Antwerp started. It was natural that his first broadcast on returning to the front should be on the "Home Thoughts From Abroad" theme. He touched a significant truth in his conclusion: "The sad thing, when you've been many years campaigning, is to come back to the front and realize that you've come home. This is the life you know best. It seems only natural and right, and even comfortable mentally, to be on a battlefield for Christmas. *This* is home."

His homecoming was at a moment of peril. The day he reached the press camp at Wijchen was the day on which the Germans launched their surprise offensive through the Ardennes, with the aim of splitting the American and British armies apart and recapturing Brussels and Antwerp. It was a cold Christmas— on the fronts, in London and at home. Halton and Lafleur, from the clammy chill of the Nijmegen Salient, and Herbert and Barette, from the similarly cold Canadian front in Italy, sent home special "Christmas-With-The-Troops" programmes. Christmas morning found London in the grip of a cold wave. But there was a deeper chill in the thought of the German advance on Brussels and Antwerp, and of the price the Belgians would pay for their welcome to their liberators.

It was a brilliantly moonlit New Year's eve when I set out to walk into the City. There was always a ghostly beauty in blacked-out London under moonlight. Through the long tunnel of the Strand and Fleet Street, I seemed to be the only person abroad, and my own echoing foosteps the only sound. But when I rounded Ludgate Circus and came to the West Front of St. Paul's Cathedral, there was a crowd on the steps. The great west doors were closed. People who had come early enough were at the watchnight service in the crypt, where all the cathedral services had to be held during the war. The impulse which had drawn these other Londoners was doubtless reverent also, but the songs they sang as they waited for the New Year concealed it. Just before midnight, while the worshippers prayed in the crypt, the crowd on the steps was singing one of the earthiest of all the service songs, and between verses came the distant drone and then the explosion of a vestigial V-1, launched from a German bomber somewhere in the moonlit sky over the North Sea.

The Ardennes offensive did not come near the Canadians, but it nevertheless brought the threat of complementary attacks on their positions in the Nijmegen Salient and along the Maas. However, the chance of battle erupting around Nijmegen faded with Montgomery's countermeasures; he had moved with sureness and skill even before Eisenhower called on him. Halton and Lafleur, who had gone to the Ardennes sector at the first news, with Lloyd Moore as their engineer, were able on the last day of the year to report that the offensive had been stopped short of the Meuse river. The three of them celebrated the New Year in Brussels, with a visit to a night club. In the early hours of New Year's morning the sound of aircraft flying low over the city brought them out to the street in time to see part of the last large-scale operation by the Luftwaffe—a series of low-level attacks on Allied airfields in Holland and eastern Belgium. It was as complete a surprise as the break-out of von Rundstedt's armies had been, and it cost the Allies scores of aircraft destroyed on the ground. Halton, Lafleur and Moore heard the bombs explode and saw the flames go up as the Germans hit the Brussels airfield.

Don Fairbairn, a corporal no longer, but commissioned, saw some of that action too. Being a combatant, he was able to play more than a spectator's part. He was at an air station in Holland, near Eindhoven, celebrating the New Year at a mess party when the attack came in. It brought the party to a sudden stop and sent all present to arms. So Don's salute to the New Year ended with a flourish as he lay on his back on a flat roof, shooting at low-flying aircraft with a sten gun. A sten gun was an improbable anti-aircraft weapon, but the planes were very low indeed so he blazed away happily.

On January 8, having won the battle, Montgomery held his unhappily-conceived press conference. He was unquestionably the hero of the occasion and the saviour, not only of much of Belgium from a savage re-occupation, but of the Allied cause from a costly and humiliating reverse. But his air of triumph so wounded some American sensitivities as to destroy his chances of exercising a decisive voice in the strategy of the eventual victory. Halton and Lafleur were at the conference, and in view of its sad consequences, Halton's report makes interesting reading now. This is what he broadcast that evening:

Field Marshal Sir Bernard Mongomery, better known as Monty, will never tell his war correspondents about the future. "Not a word, gentlemen, not a word." But he's fascinating enough just talking about the past—especially this immediate past in which the Germans smartened us up for fair and as a result of which Monty got a bigger command.

Our fine C-in-C summoned the war correspondents to meet him today. The first time since Normandy. And you hop to it when Monty calls. You drive two hundred miles for a Monty conference. There's always a story. There's always colour and humour as well as meat. And now there's high drama in the air. Monty was specially colourful today. In fact he was cute—full of quips and humour. And this time, for a change, he was wearing the uniform of a British airborne formation of which he is colonel commandant: the maroon coloured beret and the weird camouflage jacket. This time he was talking about Rundstedt instead of Rommel. Rommel was a good general, he said, but Rundstedt is a much better general. Why, he said, Rundstedt could hit Rommel for six. In fact, he said with mock seriousness, he had sent for a picture of Rundstedt so he could read his mind.

The C-in-C described how on December 16 Rundstedt attacked; obtained tactical surprise; drove a deep wedge into the First American Army and split the American forces in two. "The situation looked as if it might become awkward," he said. Awkward! "As soon as I saw what was happening, I took certain steps to assure that if the Germans got to the Meuse, they would certainly not get over it. I carried out certain movements. Then the situation began to deteriorate. General Eisenhower placed me in command of the whole northern front."

He described the delicate and complicated business of deploying the British forces into the salient without snarling the American lines of communication. "Finally," he said, "the British power was put into battle with a bang!" It was fascinating to hear the victor of Alamein, Tunis and Normandy say that this was one of the most interesting and tricky battles he had ever handled, with great issues at stake. The great issue was that had the enemy succeeded in reaching Antwerp and cutting off the British-Canadian army group, victory would have been set back for many months. "But," said Monty, "the enemy was headed off, and then he was seen off, and now he's been written off. Headed off—seen off—written off!"

He paid full and generous tribute to the American soldier. He said: "The American soldier is a brave fighting man. Steady under fire, and with that tenacity in battle which stamps the first-class fighting man. I have spent my military career with the British soldier and I have come to love him with a great love. And I have now formed a very great affection and admiration for the American soldier. I salute the brave fighting men of America—salute them. I have been given an American identity card. I am thus identified in the army of the United States, my fingerprints being registered in the war department at Washington, which is far preferable to having them registered at Scotland Yard."

Yes, Monty was cuter than ever today. But through all that, one felt his confidence and his greatness more than ever. He might not have the greatest brain in the history of generalship, but he has one of the most icy and lucid. After all, this soldier has never lost a battle. Mind you, he never throws the dice until he has them loaded. But many other generals had superiority in numbers and yet lost the battle through mistakes. Monty has never yet made a mistake. One feels now that the German threat is over and that the dice are being loaded again. Everywhere here one feels a desperate urgency to get this war over with—fast. There will be the most careful preparation, and then it will be Monty's throw.

Alas, it was not Monty's throw.

January passed without further major excitements. It was cold in Holland, where the Canadians still held the line of the Maas and the Nijmegen Salient and awaited their push into the Rhineland. It was cold in Italy, where the "last great battle" had long since merged into a repeat performance of all the earlier ones. And it was cold in London, where a rash of burst water pipes added a touch of misery to war weariness. On a freezing morning, one popular Sunday paper attempted to cheer its millions of readers with an eight-column streamer that said in huge type: "IT WAS OUR CLIMATE THAT MADE THE EMPIRE."

16–ACROSS THE RHINE

The winter of waiting was over, and the whole of the western front would soon be roaring and flaming, when Halton and Lafleur watched the opening of the battle for the Rhine. The Canadians once again bore the crucial burden of the attack, and from then on they were to be attacking without pause until the end. Matt's first broadcast of the attack into the Reichswald, held up a day for reasons of security, came on February 9.

Yesterday morning I stood in a hut south of Nijmegen, watching a western Canadian regiment go into battle from their start line. Just beside us four heavy machine guns were chattering wildly, covering the attack. Lieutenant Fred McKenna of Toronto, in charge of the section of machine guns, shouted: "We're sure pouring it to them this morning. My four machine guns have already fired two hundred and fifty belts—that's about fifty thousand bullets." Yes, we were sure pouring it to them. British and Canadian formations of the First Canadian Army were storming into the Siegfried Line in the Reichswald forest, just inside Germany, south of Nijmegen. A great, fierce and historic battle had begun.

It actually started the night before when more than seven hundred bombers droned over our heads to obliterate the German towns of Goch and Cleve. In the morning, the powerful assault began. At five o'clock, great numbers of our guns began to shoot. At ten o'clock, the assault formations and tanks were plunging forward in a shuddering, ghastly world. One has seen this often enough, and still it is appalling and wild excitement. The men crouch in the sodden clay. The hand grips the gun, and the spirit cries to the flesh: "Be strong, be strong.

At least, be strong enough!" And then they go. The western Canadian regiment went like tigers. They were piped into battle. Incredible! The wild skirling of the bagpipes, rising and falling against the monstrous diapason of the cannonade and the stuttering tattoo of many machine guns. And some of them were singing as they went!

His voice came again the next day:

It's early morning in Holland. In a few minutes I shall be driving into Germany, along roads already becoming familiar, to visit this and that British and Canadian regiment slogging along through the Siegfried Line. Last night the powerful Anglo-Canadian offensive, sweeping southeast through the Reichswald and into the Siegfried Line between the Meuse and the Rhine, was still going well and fast, and there is high excitement in the air. By last night, eighteen hundred prisoners had been taken. The German dead were strewn about their captured defences, and the German 84th Division was badly mauled. Many German villages were almost obliterated by shells and bombs. British troops were deep into the Reichswald—deep into the Siegfried Line. Our casualties were light. We hadn't lost a single prisoner. The enemy was looking dispiritedly for tactical reserves.

We've broken in. Now we are trying to break through. We've gone fast, but we'd have gone faster except for mud. This battle is now a matter of keeping a few roads open through seas of mud, to maintain the momentum of the attack. . . . The tanks and Crocodiles and Buffaloes and other huge mechanical monsters often bog themselves hopelessly down. The great beating flails on the mine-busting tanks sometimes scoop out deep holes into which the tank lugubriously falls and flounders. And on the roads themselves, the sappers and traffic control people work and shout like demons, to keep the stuff going up. The Canadian assault regiments on the left of the attack are cleaning the enemy positions out right to the banks of the river. And they're fighting under astonishing conditions. It's an amphibious operation. The whole area is flooded deep, with only the tops of villages and houses rising from the water in some places. This is supposed to be an infantry land attack. But sometimes the Canadians attack in landing craft and amphibious tanks, against objectives which are the tops of houses sticking out of the flood. Sometimes the troops clear the enemy out of their positions and have nothing to occupy but a top-storey bedroom. To get to some regiments you have to take a boat.

"From Trier on the Moselle to Holland in the north," he said on March 3, the battle for the Rhine moves to its close. Moving fast in some sectors and slow in others. Slow in ours—and hard. British troops of the Canadian First Army are linking arms on the right with men of the American Ninth Army who have raced so quickly up to meet us. Thousands of Germans are trying to get away. But here on the left, the Canadians are having a close and savage battle in and around the Hochwald, the pivot of the whole German line. To avoid disaster, the Germans have to hold that pivot until the last possible minute. And so, once more, by the fortunes of war, the Canadians are having the toughest job in the whole Allied army. They had Caen and Falaise. They had the Channel ports. They had the Scheldt Estuary. Then they had an easy winter while the British and American troops had the brunt of it. But now they've got the Hochwald fighting, and it is as hard as anything we've had anywhere. It's beautiful country down there. Thick pine woods and pleasant fields and rich farms. It *was* pleasant country, but it's a torn and reeking and bloody battlefield now. Especially in the gap in the woods. We hoped the armoured division was going to break through the other day and get in the enemy's rear and upset his whole applecart, and the tanks got the high ground, but they were stopped in the woods.

The ride between the press camp and the front grew longer each day as the attack went forward, through the Reichswald, through the bristling defences of the stretch of open country which lay beyond, and then into, and through, the Hochwald and the Hochwald gap. From his reports as they came in each day, Halton seemed to be everywhere. There were a lot of places to go. General Crerar's army was at that time a very large one, with British divisions and a Polish division under command as well as his own troops. So Matt hurried from division to division and from forward battalion to forward battalion.

"I am sorry," he said one day, "but I must take you to the Hochwald again—the Hoch*valt*, as the Germans call it. The High Wood where Canadian soldiers are now stretching their courage and endurance to the utmost, and beyond the utmost, to bring a battle to an end. When I left the battle an hour ago, an Ontario regiment was having its grimmest battle of the war in that last bloody southeast corner of the wood."

And on the day following:

"It's a thick, dark wood which will have Canadian memories

forever. The ghost of Siegfried is said to wander here, and now there are others to wander with him."

That was the last day of the Hochwald fighting. There was still terrible fighting until the west bank of the Rhine was cleared. Halton covered it, but in between battles he found time for a broadcast about First Canadian Army, which, with one armoured and two infantry divisions as its main Canadian constituents, had a larger number of British and other non-Canadian elements. He had taken note of criticism of this in some Canadian newspapers.

"Normally," he said,

only about a third of its fighting personnel is Canadian. It is sometimes asked, therefore, why Canada should have a full dress army. Is it merely for the sake of national prestige? The answer is a big "No." In any case, Canada has five divisions in the field if you include those in Italy, and five divisions make an army. But the reason we have a Canadian army in Western Europe is because the British War Office asked us to a year ago. The organization of an army and its headquarters is a complicated and elaborate and expert affair. We had one already in England. The British said: "Let's use it. Let's put British troops under Canadian Command." It's the first time that Canada has ever had an army organization in the field, with a Canadian general, Canadian staff officers and Canadian army troops. It has proved itself brilliantly."

Of General Crerar he said:

The Canadian army commander is a man of considered judgment and immense knowledge of war. He is no flaming personality. He is no McNaughton, no Montgomery, no legend discussed by soldiers in slit trenches or nicknamed "the little corporal." But he has proved, as I felt he would in a talk nearly a year ago, that he would have cool judgment and cold nerves in the hard hours when great decisions are in the scales. General Crerar is one of those forward commanders who like seeing for themselves what is going on in the battle. To do this, he gets into his little artillery observation plane and flies over the front. He does it often. He is no man of blood and iron—or blood and guts. Spend a couple of hours with him at teatime and you find a student of affairs; a man with a better idea of what's happening in the political world than some other soldiers.

The major assault across the Rhine was on March 24, and Halton's voice came triumphantly:

There was just one more river to cross, and now it is crossed. In slit trenches and in cellars in the Hochwald, I had often listened to Canadian soldiers talking about the crossing of the Rhine. The last assault crossing, and perhaps the hardest. And now it seems almost too good to be true that the Rhine is crossed. There may be hard battles ahead. But the wide, swift, symbolic German river, the very symbol of Germany, is crossed; and there's no doubt that after some days or weeks, we'll break out of our bridgeheads and rush towards victory and the end. . . .

It seems appropriate that this crossing of the Rhine should have been the most spectacular day of the whole war for us. Certainly, it was the most spectacular thing I have seen in eight years of going to see battles. Really you don't tell the story of a great operation unless you tell the story of the planning and preparation. . . . I can only tell now of what I saw in this fantastic day between six o'clock in the morning and noon, as I went up and down the banks of the Rhine between the 51st Highland Division and the 15th Scottish Division, between Calcar and Xanten. This was a time when you could see battle in all its aspects. Here were we, attacking; and over there across the Rhine, three or four hundred yards away, were the Germans.

He told of the preparatory bombing from the air; of the plans for a great—and unorthodox—airborne drop on top of the German positions after the ground troops had made their assault across the river; and of the artillery bombardment.

Listeners are probably tired of hearing about artillery programmes. But here it is. It was probably the most concentrated shoot in this war or the last. And as the thousands of guns were shooting their hundreds of thousands of shells, hundreds of bombers were unloading just across the river. There was a time when I was almost frightened by the shooting of our own guns and the explosions of our own shells and bombs. The earth was shuddering, and you could feel the blast tearing at your clothes, and wherever you looked you saw a ring of fire. . . . But then, at precisely ten o'clock, our guns stopped shooting. At one moment, the whole earth shuddering, and mad. At the next, absolute silence except for the shouting of men, the sound of assault craft clanking into the Rhine, and the occasional chatter of a machine gun. The reason for this silence, which seemed as monstrous as the din, was that the airborne were coming. The greatest airborne operation of the war was under way. The guns were forbidden to shoot now, lest they should hit any of the hundreds and hundreds of aircraft that were bringing the paratroops in, flying at only six hundred feet, to descend behind and on top of the Germans, only two or three miles away. The artillery silence meant that the Germans started shooting. . . .

First the far-off hum, and then the sky filled with troop-carrying planes. For three solid hours these planes came over our heads, and in the near distance, now that the pall of smoke was rising, we saw the thousands of brown parachutes open just above the ground—only six hundred feet. We could actually see thousands of British and American paratroops—and a Canadian battalion—dropping into the middle of the German positions behind the Rhine. For weeks we had known that this was going to happen, and that we'd be able to see it, but I hadn't realized what a fantastic thing it would be.

The troop-carrying Dakotas came over in unending streams, and as they came, tragic, spectacular things happened. There was a big Flying Fortress up there. In it were sixteen American Army photographers and observers, watching the battle. The plane was shot up by enemy flak, and nine or ten of the men in it got out by parachute. Then the plane soared up and down the sky for half an hour, diving and banking and wheeling, a great machine suddenly gone mad. It crashed at last in flames. A few minutes later one of the Dakotas, coming back from the other side, and damaged by flak, burst into flame. It came moaning and screaming down and hit the ground in a group of houses two hundred yards from where I stood. That was a really terrifying moment.

The air armada came from bases in England, and included hundreds of gliders towed by bombers, as well as the paratroop-carrying Dakotas which Halton watched. The offer of a ride in a towing plane had come from the Air Ministry, via Canadian Military Headquarters, to our office in London, and as I was the only one there free to go, I accepted it. Thus, having left an office desk a couple of days earlier for an air station from which part of the force was to fly, I got my own view of the Rhine crossing from a Halifax bomber named Queenie, which towed a glider carrying medical supplies. Her crew had been together in two sorties through the flak at Arnhem, and their luck, and that of the glider pilot, held through this last airborne operation of the war. But my view over the dropping zone was brief. There was a lot of fire coming up from the ground, and as a cloud of gliders descended, a shell hit one of Queenie's wings, knocking out an engine and an aileron. Fortunately it was the starboard aileron, for the turn which we had to make to safety was to port. The captain got us up out of our dive by a magnificent piece of flying, so we got precariously back to England.

There was a lot that I still wanted to say when I had finished my broadcast that night. I tried a couple of nights later:

When you know you're going to see a tremendous spectacle like that, you're apt to form pictures of it ahead of time. I know I had my preconceived pictures from the day I was promised a ride in a towing plane. I knew it would feel magnificent to be part of a skyful of aircraft, and it did. I knew we'd look like a huge sea convoy, only more so, as we paraded across a good slice of western Europe, and that was very much the way we did look. But that was background stuff. The all-important thing to see would be on the other side of the Rhine, where the gliders would cast off and sail down through the flak—gliders packed full of fighting men who still had to wait passively on chance right up to the last second. And that was a picture that wouldn't focus clearly beforehand, that would have to be seen.

Well, I did see it, and the picture's clear enough now. The principal thing in it is a circle of sky turned black by a flock of huge dark birds wheeling in beautiful and terrifying patterns. And mixed in with that picture there are others. There's a stretch of ground, scrubby-looking with growth, that still looked meaningless and irrelevant when it was rushing up to meet us. And there are the faces I couldn't see, but still *could* see through the voices that came sharp and overlapping on the intercom; the faces of six men not sure that these weren't their last seconds, but remaining completely competent. I was up in the nose, but I could see Ernie Dreaver, the tall dark Saskatchewan boy, as he sat at his guns in the rear turret and cursed because he couldn't get a shot at the flak gunners down below. I could see Gerry Varnum, although he was back of me in the pilot's seat, as the Halifax Q, Queenie gave a tremendous upward leap away from the flak. And their voices were enough for me to see the other two Canadians, Ernie Papp and Bill Hornell, and the two English lads, Len Cox and Ron Stevens, as they looked along the wing a shell had hit and appraised our chances. Maybe I didn't see them in all that detail, but they are the clearest memory now of a few moments whose measure I don't know.

You must have had your thoughts and wonderings about the men up there sometimes when you've heard a big aircraft overhead. I had often. Now I've an idea. They laugh and joke as they work. And I know part of the way of the moment that comes to some of them. I think I can guess the rest of the way. They are the masters of themselves. There are pictures of our return, too. "We'll take her as far as we can," said Gerry Varnum, sharply and finally, when he'd got Queenie up, out of her dive and out of the flak, and had found that her starboard aileron wouldn't work, and was wondering how the undercarriage was. He called for reports from this man and that, and he kept Queenie going fast and high. Someone spotted a vapour trail. "I hope it's a V-2 and not a German jet," he said. "We're not in any shape for evasive action." A little later Ernie Dreaver spoke up from the rear turret:

"There's a Halifax coming up to formate with us."

"Good show," said Gerry Varnum.

"He's going up to take a look at our wing," said Ernie.

"Good show," said Gerry.

Silence and then: "Where's that Halifax now?"

"Right along, formating with us," said Ernie.

"GOOD SHOW," said Gerry.

Conversation over the intercom eased back to normal, and then there was a shout from Ron Stevens, the English engineer: "Oh, what my mother'd say if she knew where I'd been to-day!"

"Won't she guess?" someone asked.

"They don't know at home that I do this sort of thing," said Ron. "I always tell 'em I'm still training. No use worrying people."

Yes, there's such heroic consideration as that in an airman's make-up.

Marcel Ouimet got back to the war in time for the Rhine crossing. He would have been back sooner, but after his leave he had been roped in for speaking engagements, and then for a trip to Detroit with Gregory Clark to make a film for the current Victory Loan campaign. He came in time for a close call. He crossed the river with the assault brigade of the 3rd Division, the 9th. He went ashore at the little town of Wesel, and was making his way past a block of houses with the care of an experienced campaigner when a soldier of the Highland Light Infantry asked him for a light. The soldier of course was wearing a steel helmet. Marcel was not, but had on his forage cap. He disliked steel helmets and found a forage cap much more comfortable, but in addition to being against orders, it had the disadvantage of making him look like an officer. As he held the lighter to the soldier's cigarette, the soldier fell dead at his feet with a sniper's bullet through the temple.

"I simply ran for my life," Marcel relates.

I knew the moment I saw the little hole in the man's temple that there was nothing I could do for him. I most probably established a record for the five hundred yards. Then all of a sudden I stopped, and said to myself: "What the hell are you doing, running like this?" But to this day I believe that the sniper was not shooting at the man in the steel helmet, but at the man in the forage cap. And I was just scared stiff. I don't think many war correspondents had the temper of heroes, and there was nothing more useless than a dead war correspondent. On top of this we knew that the war was close to an end, and like a lot of other people we were beginning to look over our shoulders. We would have felt rather silly getting killed in the last few weeks, or the last three or four days, as happened unfortunately to some of our best friends.

He got away, but he was to have a certain ordeal of suspense, not simply in the last days, but in the last hours of fighting.

17 – THE END APPROACHES

London, at the end of March, 1945, and for the first time since 1940, was a peaceful place. The barrage was heard no more, because raids by manned aircraft had ceased long since. The last V-2 had fallen, and the only sound from the skies now was that of our own aircraft. That could be impressive, though. One night in those last weeks of the war the sleeping city was awakened by an enormous drumming that seemed to go on for hours. It was the bomber force of one of our last mass raids on Germany, making its rendezvous over London. Some high air force commander had had the idea of giving Londoners a treat. It didn't happen again. Someone at a much greater height than the infatuated air commander had uttered a thundering order. There were too many people in hospitals, and too many people with memories of terror from the skies, for such nonsense as massing hundreds of fully-laden bombers in close manoeuvre over the city.

There was a new or at least long-unfamiliar sight in the West End—the occasional soldier wearing the red shoulder patches of the 1st Division. The Canadians had left Italy, in a move so secret that the Germans had no inkling of it until they found that they were fighting units of the 1st Canadian Corps in Holland. The news about the Canadians in Italy had been overshadowed all through the fall and winter by that of the greater and nearer battles, though they had been through fighting as fierce and weather as foul as their fellow Canadians in North-

163

west Europe. But overshadowed or not, their battles had been faithfully recorded from day to day and from month to month, first by Peter Stursberg and Benoit Lafleur and later by Bill Herbert and Paul Barette. Their broadcasts had recounted battles, large and small, all the way from the entrance to the Lombardy Plain to the final positions along the Senio River. The last Canadian action in Italy had been on the night of February 24, when two regiments of the 2nd Brigade beat off attacks on their positions. Herbert recorded the story, but censorship held it up for two months. The broadcast ended, when it did reach the air:

And so when the last record of the war is compiled, you'll find a note somewhere that the honour of fighting the final battle in Italy fell to two units which had covered themselves with glory: in the summer of '43 when they entered the Mediterranean lists; from Sicily through Ortona and the Gothic and Hitler Lines right up to Bagnacavallo— the Loyal Edmonton Regiment and the Seaforth Highlanders of Canada.

Bill was wrong in one particular. In the official history of the Canadians in Italy, the account of the battle is no small note but a part of the text.

When the censors let the broadcast go out, they also released Herbert's story of the move from Italy. The transfer of an army corps numbering some 60,000 had begun on February 13 to be completed by the end of March. Herbert, Barette and their engineer Joseph Beauregard came out among the last troops to leave.

"As far as I can learn," Herbert said,

not a single Canadian soldier, vehicle or piece of equipment was lost, stolen or strayed in the transfer of the First Canadian Division from the Eighth Army's Adriatic front to the western theatre. . . . I travelled with a brigade of the First Division. We concentrated on the Adriatic coast somewhere south of Ravenna. Here all Canadian markings on vehicles were painted out. Divisional and regimental flashes came down. Patches were removed from uniforms. The soldiers became anonymous. Then the long haul to the east coast began. Convoys of anywhere up to eighty-eight vehicles clogged the road. Our trucks crawled along at anywhere from twelve to fifteen miles an hour. It was hot and dusty, but steadily, and with minor breakdowns here and there, the brigade moved over the mountains towards the embarkation point. Camps had been set up a hundred miles or so apart. These we hit nightly. Within a few minutes at each camp, phone connections had been made with Corps headquarters, and the troops were sitting down to a hot meal. So it went day by day, until at last we reached the port, and boarded LST's and landed in the south of France.

The correspondents had to play their part in the secrecy and deception that surrounded the move. Canadian Army Public Relations kept its headquarters going, and kept publishing the Italian edition of *The Maple Leaf*, the Canadian Army's paper. Stories over the signatures of correspondents still supposedly in Italy continued to reach their newspapers and news agencies, the stories and signatures alike being supplied by P.R. staff. (Fortunately no-one tried to impersonate Herbert or Barette at a microphone). Before they left, the correspondents were given instructions: "Tell them you're on your holidays. Tell them you've been transferred to another theatre. Tell them you're on a facility visit to the western front. In fact, tell them anything but what's really going on."

"We followed the convoy lines from Marseilles to Paris," Herbert related,

checking all along the way to find out how well security was being kept. There was no trace of anything distinctly Canadian anywhere along the route. Security boxes were burned. Soldiers were not allowed to speak to French civilians. We stopped off for lunch at a wayside place, and a young French girl came over to speak to us. She told us that a great many soldiers, all of them wearing English uniforms, had been moving steadily through her village. They were the first English soldiers she had ever seen. Because Paul Barette was the only one of us who could speak French, he acted as interpreter. Later Paul told me that the girl suspected we were a party of students from an English university, inspecting the battle areas of France under our young French professor. Barette is now "the professor" to everyone.

On the main front, with the Rhine crossed and a flood of troops and weapons pouring across it over newly-made bridges, the big news had been the drive into Germany. But the Canadians, having played their crucial part in the battle for the Rhine, had been ordered away to the less spectacular but more arduous task, the liberation of Holland.

It was many months since Halton and Ouimet had first seen "the stolid Dutch dancing in the streets," and the blossoming of orange skirts and hair ribbons in liberated towns and villages. But that had been in the narrow southern strip of the country. By far the greater area and all the principal cities of Holland were still under occupation, the German command was still threatening to inundate the whole country by breaching the sea dykes, and most of the population was near starvation. That was the situation the Canadians had to deal with, so while their colleagues with the British and American armies went joyously off in to Germany in the wake of the fast driving armour, the correspondents with the Canadian Army turned north, and in what seemed the very hour of victory, were once again describing close and costly battle.

Halton was broadcasting on April 3rd:

The German war, in the words of a senior Canadian officer, has now become a silly tragedy. In previous wars, when a country saw that the game was up, they asked for terms. Germany knows now that the game is up. The German people know and the German army knows. But the German government is a pack of cornered rats sweating for their own lives. And at their service they have thousands of fanatical young Nazis who will fight as long as Hitler asks. This means that we will have to occupy and clean out every village and corner in Germany as long as there is one little group of paratroopers or Hitler youth waiting behind a road block. It means that the greatest war in history will end in a stupid anti-climax.

A week later, one of his broadcasts opened:

Just another day at the front, watching the crazy and tragic incidents of war. The Canadians storming across the river in assault craft to get at the paratroopers. The drifting white smoke of the smoke screen, the choking black smoke from the burning petrol. The tantalizingly slow, exciting ride over the new bridge as the shells go over. The exhausted sergeant of Engineers, trying to tell you that it wasn't so bad putting the bridge in under fire. . . . Just another day at the front. One of my colleagues says the public is no longer interested in this kind of thing. His editor says so in a cable. The people don't want battle, they want news of victory. But all I've got is battle.

The ruin enveloping Germany was a great preoccupation of those days. Halton and Ouimet took their first day's leave from their assignment with the Canadians to visit British and American troops in Munster. "Today," Halton said,

we saw the burning and smouldering ruins of Munster, one of Germany's oldest towns. Hitler said in 1940 that he'd hold the peace conference in Munster. In Munster he was going to lay down the fate of the world for a thousand years. Today, however, British armoured regiments, fighting hand in hand with American paratroops, cleaned the last of the Nazi paratroops out of the old city. And it's the fate of Germany that was being settled for a thousand years. Or at least, we hope, for a century or two.

The troops were overrunning concentration camps and uncovering repetitive evidence of Gestapo and SS devilishness. Thus Halton from Zutphen, "the old Dutch town which Sir Philip Sidney made immortal."

"The Nazis are now calling themselves werewolves," Halton said. "They are worse than that. The Nazis and the Gestapo are passing from the stage of Europe, but even as they go they leave a trail of slime and abominable crime. I saw one of these crimes today."

He went on to tell of ten Dutchmen, dead from torture, whose bodies the fleeing Gestapo had left under a hasty covering of earth. They were now being given proper burial, their graves being dug by German paratroopers taken prisoner in the battle just over. He looked at the bodies. "I saw and was sick," he said.

Some of the paratroopers dug graves while others lay utterly exhausted on the grass after a gruelling battle. I looked them over and then spoke to one of them. I pointed to the ten Dutchmen and said: "What do you think of this?" The young, unshaven, red-eyed paratrooper rose to his feet and stood, shaking, at attention. "Das ist ein schweinerei" ('it's a swinish thing"), he said in a trembling voice.

"Who did it?' I went on.

"Not us, not us," he said. "We didn't do it. We are soldiers. The Gestapo did it."

A couple of weeks later Halton was broadcasting from the

North German town of Meppen, within a thirty-mile radius of which there were six concentration camps and political prisons, and several prisoner-of-war camps. He spoke of 2,000 Russians in one of the prisoner-of-war camps, most of them dying.

We came too late to save them. . . . In another camp which I saw, there are twelve thousand Italians in the same condition. When Italy went out of the war these Italian soldiers came over to our side, and were captured by the Germans. They're not human beings any more, to look at. . . . All round there were apple trees in blossom, and a dozen different kinds of birds were singing. How can birds sing here? It seems impossible. Almost a blasphemy."

But he added: "It's well to remember that tens of thousands of the people the Nazis have tortured and murdered were Germans. German heroes who would not recant, for whom the worst tortures were reserved. They are the proof that not all Germans are Nazis."

There were other preoccupations: the twin threat of starvation and inundation that overhung the Dutch; the Goebbels propaganda that the German population would take to guerilla warfare and shoot from behind every tree if the armies collapsed; the strange myth of a last stand by Hitler with half a million Nazis in the mountain fastnesses of southern Germany, which somehow possessed Allied Supreme Headquarters almost to the last; and above all the sheer fatigue of an enormous front and the tumble of swiftly moving events. On April 16 Halton explained, as far as security allowed, the disposition of the Canadian Army. He could not mention the presence of the 1st Canadian Corps in Holland, so his picture was of necessity incomplete.

"The Canadian Army presses on," he said,

on the right, the Fourth Canadian Armoured Division moving against increasing opposition towards Emden. Then reading from right to left, the Polish Armoured Division moves north along the east bank of the Ems River, parallel to the Second Canadian Infantry Division west of the river. On this front, Canadian armoured cars today reached the North Sea. The Third Division, further west, have taken Zwolle and Meppen, and Canadians are fighting hard today for the town of Appeldoorn, and on the left, British troops of this powerful army have taken Arnhem. So the German garrisons in western Holland are now cut off.

He went on to talk of the famine in Holland and the dilemma it created for the Canadians:

The Canadian Army will now have to turn around and strike westward, if that is its plan, to clean the Germans out of the great suffering cities of Amsterdam and Rotterdam and the rest, where men, women and children are dying of hunger and disease. A tragic dilemma may face the Canadians. If they strike fast and hard, using their artillery and bombers and rockets to reduce the German garrisons, Dutch cities will be broken and torn, and Dutch civilians will die. If they move cautiously, the war will drag on for extra days and weeks, and Dutch civilians will still die, of starvation."

The dilemma was to be solved, in the nick of time, by the successful negotiations with the Germans for the admission of food, and the almost immediately ensuing German surrender.

"The vast mass of the German people want to quit," Halton broadcast on April 19.

The German High Command wanted to quit last July. But the fierce black fever of Nazism keeps this odd country fighting. Not for nothing did Hitler take the best youth of Germany and turn them into inhuman fighting machines for his elite SS and paratroop divisions. Believe me, it's not pleasant for the soldiers to hear every day that the battle is over, to hear about the preparations being made everywhere for V Day, and then to have to go into battle again. It's hard to die now, and I am moved with deep admiration every time I visit the fighting men, to see them do the job as gallantly today as yesterday. I personally take fewer chances than I used to, but the fighting men go right on against this black fever of the Nazis, who still fight hard here and there. I drove hundreds of miles today, from the Canadian Third Division in Holland to the British now fighting in the outskirts of Bremen, and wherever I went I heard of fierce fighting.

In another broadcast on the same day:

Dismay runs through Holland today, as the news passes from village to village and from man to man: the Germans have blown the great sea wall. For a hundred and fifty years the Dutch have feared this news, and now here it is. It's the story of a crime. The Germans have blown the dykes at the western end of the giant causeway across the Zuider Zee. The waters of the sea are now surging wildly in great waves that travel faster than a farmer's wife can run, over hundreds of square miles to reach land which the hard-working Dutch had reclaimed from the ocean in four hundred years. The work and devotion of generations and centuries of man has been wantonly undone by high explosives in the hands of a few Germans. Scores of towns and villages are in the path of the flood. It's already certain that this black deed is disastrous for Holland. We'll know soon enough whether it's catastrophic.

Halton and Ouimet were forbidden until April 23, by the same censorship blackout that had held up the reports of the move from Italy, to mention the presence of the 1st Corps in Holland. When they did, it was to talk of the 1st Division with some sadness.

My first meeting with the First Division, said Halton, was in the early morning of December 19th, 1939, when they landed in Glasgow. I remember how Britain was cheered the next day when people read that history was repeating itself and that the first Canadian contingent had arrived. Seeing the red patch here now, it seemed a long time since we saw it in the white dust and blinding heat of the Sicilian mountains when the division was the hard-hitting left hook of the Eighth Army. And a long time since that hot smokey dawn of September 3rd, 1943, when they and a British division crossed the Strait of Messina and made the first breach in the fortress of mainland Europe. The division has had a long, hard grind since then: on the Moro River, at Ortona, in the Hitler Line and the Gothic Line; and I don't find too many familiar faces when I visit the old units.

Marcel sent a hurried note across to me on April 25:

V Day may be near but we haven't got that impression over here now. Hard fighting still lies ahead. But we will have a better appreciation of the situation once the Russians have cracked through. We are moving to Germany tomorrow, to the advance camp. This has been one of the hardest campaigns to cover. The front has been so wide. I travel as much as 240 miles some days, never less than 150 miles.

Matt Halton, raising the mileage a little, broadcast:

We live in the jeep. We drive as much as 200 miles forward to get a story, and after an hour up there we have to come back 200 miles to get the story out. And the jeep is a tough little mustang. But fortunately we're getting calloused in the right places. On a fixed battlefront, you can drive from Army headquarters to the front line in an hour. But now you leave Army and pass the Corps headquarters, and the traffic thins out. And then you're driving through miles and miles of villages and forest and farmland, where there's not an army vehicle to be seen. You race along a lonely forest road, alert, uncomfortable. The fighting units have gone through, but you may be ambushed by paratroopers or sniped at. You round a corner and see two or three German soldiers, your heart stops, and you see they have their hands in the air. They're asking to surrender, but you can't be bothered with prisoners, and on you go. I've never been sniped at yet, but I always sigh with relief when I see some of our own vehicles and find myself among soldiers again—our soldiers—and I wish somebody would give me an armoured car.

But the great sensation these days is exhilaration. How often we've dreamed of this. In the long dark nights of the London Blitz, in the jungles of Burma, in the dreary sandstorms or blinding heat of the Libyan desert, in the white dust of Sicily, and in the cold bloody winter on the Moro River in Italy. And then in Normandy when it seemed that the SS divisions would never crack. I've looked forward to this day, and now here we go through the ruins of Germany. The rich farmlands and pleasant villages of Germany have escaped destruction. Germany's a beautiful country, spacious and massive. You see no obvious need for more *lebensraum*. It's a clean, well-ordered country, the buildings are solid and strong. And you think what a great people the Germans could have been if they hadn't had a demon in them. And to see them now, you wouldn't think they had a demon in them.

Some of them are grim, but thousands of them want to be friendly. They're obviously glad it's over and they show no rancour; that's the simple fact of the case. Often we go to a farmhouse and ask for eggs, offering cigarettes or chocolate in exchange, and often they press us to take more eggs than we ask for. They often offer us cakes and meat. Sometimes, far from home, we have to find a billet for the night. We knock at the door of a German house, they give us rooms and huge beds, with those thick German feather beds. And we sleep in the same house with them, never thinking of werewolves or knives in the dark.

Your hate rises of course when you see, as I saw the other day, Dutchmen who had been tortured to death. And it rises again when you see the streams of freed slaves thronging down the roads. This astonishing sight is one we see every day. In the areas we've already overrun in Germany we've liberated over a million of these slaves, chiefly Russian and Polish but also French, Czechs, Yugoslavs and others. We've seen them in bands of several hundred at a time. They're not always emaciated, starving, ragged. Sometimes you wouldn't know they were slaves, except for their language, and the fact that they're laughing and chattering away, and waving and singing. But I've seen others, hungry, and even barefooted, mad with hate of the Germans, looting shops for food and clothes. What an extraordinary thing this is, in the twentieth century. You see these things and wonder if you're not back in the pages of an historical novel, back in the Thirty Years' War. Freed bondsmen—ten or twelve million men and women of Europe have been uprooted by the Germans and enslaved.

The Berchtesgaden Redoubt myth was current to the end. Halton broadcast on April 25:

The Americans and the Russians are at last face to face. Berlin is in flames and almost surrounded, and half of it is captured. But even now it's not the end. Once we thought that these two titanic events, the taking of Berlin and the link with the Russians, would bring the curtain down on the great drama. But we know now that a strange fierce epilogue is still to be played. We know that Hitler and at least half a million of his elite troops are going to fight to the last in the Berchtesgaden Redoubt. Dramatic news, yes. But it's bad news. There will be a hard and costly battle to clean these cornered rats out of the mountains south of Salzberg where Germany, Austria and Switzerland meet. The Nazis mean to hold out as long as they can in the north—in northern Germany, Denmark and Norway. In Norway alone they still have ten divisions, but the main stronghold is the Berchtesgaden Redoubt. Even now the majority of the German troops are no longer facing the Russians or the western Allies. Of the Germans bearing arms today, the best troops are already in the south.

It was to be only nine days before Doenitz surrendered all the Germans in Holland, Denmark, and North Germany to Montgomery, and when the Allies reached Berchtesgaden they found only a frightened caretaker. But the fear was real and very official when Matt spoke.

The threat of Dutch starvation, as we have seen, was lifted at the last minute when the German Reichskommissar of Holland, Arthur Seyss-Inquart, agreed at an extraordinary conference in a village schoolhouse in occupied Holland with

Eisenhower's chief of staff, General Bedell Smith, to let in food for the population. We got the story of that from Peter Stursberg. After his last stint on the Italian front, Stursberg had left the CBC and gone to work for the London *Daily Herald*. The *Herald* had sent him to Holland for the last weeks of the war, and he seized every opportunity of rejoining old colleagues at the microphone. He managed to be one of the only two correspondents at the conference. He and his companion were not allowed into the room, but they could watch the proceedings through a glass door from the hall where they waited.

"We were so close," Stursberg said,

that I almost bumped into Seyss-Inquart when he came into the hallway during the luncheon break. He limped past me to the room where the Germans were to eat. A heavy, almost gross man, wearing thick glasses, the *gauleiter* look baffled and beaten, and I couldn't help wondering if this was the same Nazi who had turned Austria over to Hitler and had run Holland like a feudal province.

The delegates from the German side included several Dutch representatives. "They were mostly civil servants of the former Netherlands government," Stursberg said, "who had stayed in office because someone had to run the country. They were no collaborators."

Seyss-Inquart was accompanied by his Dutch collaborator lieutenant, the Reichsrichter of Holland:

"The Reichsrichter," Stursberg said,

looked like no Dutch I have ever seen. He was a great coarse man with a huge bulbous nose. The tremendous nose perspired visibly whenever he was agitated, which seemed to be every time Seyss-Inquart peered at him through his glasses. The two men, so strikingly overfed, compared with the gaunt drawn figures of the Dutch representatives whom they had brought to the conference, seemed to me to be the very embodiment of all Nazi ugliness.

The link-up of the Americans and the Rusians at Torgau, on the Elbe, caused Matt Halton to write ruefully that while the Russians were free to come over to our side, we were not free to go over to theirs, and Marcel Ouimet to observe in a broadcast that the Russians were strange allies.

"If I had had Churchill's imagination," Marcel said many

years later, "I could have coined the phrase: 'An iron curtain has descended.' Unfortunately I did not have Churchill's imagination so I did not coin the phrase. But the iron curtain descended at the end of April, 1945."

Its descent was attended with, or preceded by, a resounding party with the Russians at Torgau which Halton, Ouimet and Moore attended. Their survival can be attributed in the first place to magnificent digestive systems and in the second to Marcel's ability, even under extreme difficulties, to read road signs. The ordeal started when the CBC trio, with their conducting officer and a driver—not Bill Williamson this time—set out from the Canadian advanced press camp at Meppen for Nurnberg, where they were to make rendezvous with other correspondents of various western nationalities and the staff of General Hodges' US First Army. Five men were a large load for a long slow journey in a jeep, and the journey was long and slow, because the autobahn was too badly cratered to travel on and they had to make constant detours. They were all packed into the jeep because they could not take the van. Word had come that the Russians would allow only one recording van on their side of the Elbe, so it had been agreed that this should be the BBC's. The BBC's vans had only one turntable apiece, and thus could not provide continuous recording like the CBC's, but this did not make much difference, considering the amount of recording that was done on that day.

They left Nurnberg the next morning before it was light, got to the western end of the bridge at Torgau about 5:00 a.m., and were kept waiting till nearly noon before being allowed to cross.

"There was a beautiful blonde Russian girl, with a tommy gun, guarding the bridge," says Moore. "Anyone setting foot on that bridge would probably have been dead very quickly."

With their conducting officers and drivers, the war correspondents' group numbered some forty or fifty. When they were allowed to cross, they had to jam five or six in a jeep. According to Moore, this was because the Russians wanted their western allies to appear short of transport. Once across the bridge and on the road to the castle where they were to be entertained, the correspondents saw Russian tommy gunners fifty yards apart on either side of the road.

They got to the castle, formerly the property of a general of the Luftwaffe. But here let Marcel take up the story:

We were ushered into an ante-room, handed Russian cigarettes, which we found strange because they were only half filled with tobacco, the rest being filter, and offered sherry. We thought: "This is not what we used to read about the days of the Czars." But within minutes the doors were thrown open into a huge room, where a dining table was set out in U shape. We were a large party: some correspondents, Belgian, French, US, British and Canadian, and their conducting officers; the staff of the First US Army, and the staff of the Soviet Fifth Guards Armoured Army, which had fought at Stalingrad. At each place at the table were a bottle of vodka and a bottle of champagne. And I remember Matt Halton, sitting opposite me, saying: "I'm not going to try to fight this one." And he was among the first casualties.

Everyone was a casualty before the lunch was over. Marcel explains:

On top of this, mind you, there was wine—flowing. There was a head table and there was a toastmaster. The first toast was to the memory of President Roosevelt, who had died some twelve or thirteen days before. The second was to Winston Churchill. Practically none of us spoke Russian, but five or six of the Soviet officers spoke either English or French. I happened to be sitting next to a Russian colonel who spoke some French.

When the toasts started, knowing that we were in for a long session, I just touched my lips to the vodka, drinking to the memory of Roosevelt and the health of Churchill. But at that point the Russian colonel said to me: "You know the Russian custom, when drinking a toast, is to empty the glass." And at that moment the toastmaster called for a toast to Stalin, so figuring that it was the gesture, I emptied my glass. And from 12:30 or one o'clock I counted twenty-seven such toasts, to the point that we got up from the table at about 5:30 in the afternoon.

It is wonderful that anyone should remember anything of that afternoon, but Moore recalls that there were Cossack dancers and an orchestra. And Ouimet adds:

"We were the people who looked like the army of the proletariat, because we were all in battledress, while our hosts were all in full dress uniforms, complete with hip boots, well shined."

But still Marcel enjoyed a sartorial triumph. Some weeks previously he had gone to cover an action by a Canadian tank brigade, and had been given a tank coverall. He had worn this to the reception.

"And my last recollection as I left the party," he says, "is of two Russian generals helping me into this coverall and playing with the zippers, which went from the ankles right up to the neck. They'd never seen this kind of thing before."

They piled into their jeep, crossed the Elbe and got on to the autobahn for the run back to Nurnberg. They were to be surprised.

"We figured," says Marcel,

that our driver at any rate would be sober. But while we were being entertained, the Russians had been entertaining our drivers. And after a while, when I looked around, I saw a road sign that said: "Berlin, twelve kilometers." Whereupon I got rather nervous. Our conducting officer was Captain Phil Lauzon. I tapped him on the shoulder and said: "Look, my friend, where's your map?"

Lauzon said: "I never carry a map. I go by the stars."

I said: "You're going straight into Berlin, and at sixty miles an hour."

He said: "I don't give a damn, I'm responsible for your safety, I'm responsible for this jeep, and I'm in command of this jeep." Remember, he'd been at the party too.

Then I saw: Berlin—seven kilometres" so I grabbed the driver and said: "You bloody well stop!" Because Berlin had not been taken at that time, and most probably we would have ended up, having feted the link-up of the Americans with the Russians, in a prisoner-of-war camp if not worse off. But reason prevailed, and we turned back to Nurnberg.

Some time the next morning in the house where he was billeted with Matt, Lloyd, Phil Lauzon and some other correspondents and conducting officers, Marcel awoke and said to Matt, already but very recently awake:

"What happened?"

"We had a party with the Russians," said Matt. Then he looked for his watch. It was gone. They made a canvass among the other correspondents later in the morning, and found that some half-dozen watches, along with a few cigarette lighters and similar trifles were missing. Marcel still had his own incidental property, however. Before going to Torgau he had been warned by a Belgian correspondent, and had put his watch, lighter and camera in the breast pocket of his battledress jacket, and buttoned it.

"But to this day I would not accuse our hosts of any pilfering," he says.

I suspect that at one point we were in a mood for exchanging. Matt, for instance, found in his pocket two little red stars, made of tin, which a Russian general had given him for a souvenir. I suppose these red stars were worth about twenty cents each—and Matt's watch was a quite expensive Gruen. It just shows the atmosphere that prevailed.

But it was the last time we were allowed across the Elbe without a pass. The Soviet military people and correspondents were perfectly welcome in our messes. People like Ilya Ehrenburg, the famous writer, and Konstantin Simonov, the man who wrote *Days and Nights*, the story of the defence of Stalingrad, could come freely on our side, but we weren't allowed on theirs without passes. Years later I talked about this with Ehrenburg, and told him I couldn't understand how this had developed. Neither could he. But later he alluded to this conversation in one of a series of articles that he wrote, and called me a fascist.

18 – THE LAST DAY

The shooting stopped on the western front on the night of May 4. May 4 was not the last day of the war in Europe. That was not until May 7, when General Eisenhower accepted the surrender of all German armed forces at Rheims. But it was on the evening of May 4 that Field Marshal Montgomery took the surrender of all German forces in Holland, Northwest Germany and Denmark, and that word of the capitulation reached the front. Hostilities were to cease at eight o'clock the next morning, but the cessation did not wait for morning.

So May 4 was really the last day. It found Ouimet and Halton, not by chance, far inside Northwest Germany, with the regiments they had landed with on D Day; and it found Ouimet committed to go over the top with the Régiment de la Chaudière in an attack at eleven o'clock that night if the war was still on by then. Marcel reported in English as well as in French the next day. His broadcast opened with one of the cleanest of the many recordings of gunfire that CBC engineers had made from Italy onwards. Then he tolled out his sentences:

A few thousand yards away from Emden, one of Germany's main seaports, that's what Canadian guns sounded like last night. From the 13th Field Regiment's twenty-five pounders, the last salvoes were being fired. The last cry; the last belch of smoke and steel from guns which had never ceased thundering for months. The shells whipped the air, and there was a distant roar in the direction of the enemy's lines; a few explosions followed by a complete silence. Only the whistling of the wind through the tree-tops and the beating of the rain against the window panes could break it. And at the command post of the Chaudière regiment, where I spent the last twelve hours of the war on the Canadian front, we had listened to the guns with emotion, almost with religious fervour. It seemed so much that with their loud booming voices they wanted to proclaim victory ahead of the church bells.

The Chaudières' command post was a little distance away from the town of Aurich. When I reached it, the colonel and some of his officers were awaiting orders from Brigadier Roberts, officer commanding the Eighth Brigade. He'd been in Aurich since one o'clock, and it was now four in the afternoon. Negotiating with the Germans, he was trying to persuade them that resistance was futile—absolutely useless. "As soon as Aurich is cleared," the colonel explained, "my battalion will go through and we'll take positions on the road to Emden." But, he went on with a grin, what had the correspondents to say about the end of the war?

I took a very serious attitude in reply: "It should be over tonight or in the morning, sir."

"I'm sure you're kidding," the colonel said, and his second-in-command and one of his company commanders seemed to be thinking along the same lines. Still, I was only repeating what a staff officer had told us the night before at Canadian Army Headquarters.

The second-in-command, Major Lespérance of Montreal, heard my explanation, but it seemed he couldn't accept it.

"It's easy," he said, "to have such ideas in the rear areas. But I would like to know who will clear Emden. They've got plenty of guns in there."

I mentioned the word "capitulation," but the officers weren't any more convinced. Not because they'd had so much resistance in the last few days, but because of the thorough demolition job which the enemy was practising all along the roads. "He's using thousand-pound bombs and torpedoes from the Emden arsenal to crater the roads. There's a crater every hundred feet or so, and to span some of them we need Bailey bridges. Come along," said Colonel Taschereau, "we'll show you." We got into his jeep and drove about a mile along the road. The O.C. had not exaggerated. The pioneers and the engineers were very busy indeed, and they weren't sparing their efforts to allow our vehicles to pass. But the lieutenant from the Provost Corps warned against driving any further than a certain point. "The Boche is in that house a hundred yards away," he said. "There has been a truce since one o'clock, but somehow, two Queen's Own riflemen have just been killed. And for your information, sir," he went on, looking at the colonel, "you've just missed two mines on the road with your jeep."

We decided to turn back. As we reached the first crater, we had the unusual sight of four motorcycles advancing towards us, two of them mounted by our own officers, the other two by German officers carrying a white flag. They were just back from the Third Division's headquarters, where their negotiations had taken place. They looked tired and they looked very depressed. They seemed ill at ease and far from ready to smile, even when some of our boys had to give their motorcycles a push along the edge of the crater.

Back at the command post I told Colonel Taschereau I had another five-hour jeep drive ahead of me and that I should get back to camp without any delay. "You're staying with us," he said. "You claim the war will be over tonight. We sincerely doubt it. We believe we'll be attacking in a few hours, and I'd like you to wait until tomorrow before returning. If we attack, you come in with us. If it's victory, we'll have a drink together. Either way, you'll be with the same unit as on D Day."

So Marcel stayed, to take part in either the eleven o'clock attack or the celebration. Matt could not stay. He had to make the five-hour journey back to camp because he expected a call to Rheims and the final surrender. He never got to Rheims, because there was too much to do closer at hand. But he took up his colleague's story in one of his broadcasts next day. His account and Marcel's differ as to the time that word of the cease-fire reached the front, but between them they give a sufficient picture of what it was like.

"At ten o'clock on Friday night, Canadian regiments were in battle," Halton said.

In the Third Canadian Division, some of the regiments that were in action, or waiting to go into action, near the German town of Aurich, were the Queen's Own Rifles, the Regiment of the Chaudière, the Highland Light Infantry and the North Nova Scotia Highlanders. The Chaudière were at the top of their form, and they had been for several weeks. "I don't know how they do it," the brigadier told me. "You can't hold them. They do their attacking on the run."

But the Chaudière too were getting sick of the long drawn-out battle and the incessant shelling. And now on Friday night, at ten o'clock, they were waiting to go in and attack an enemy strong point at eleven o'clock. In battalion headquarters they were listening to the radio. They heard the BBC programme interrupted by an announcement from Supreme Headquarters. Accustomed only to death and suffering, they now heard the voice say that the German armies had surrendered. In other words, they did not have to attack. They had done their last attack.

At one moment the voices on the Canadian Second Corps' radio sets were saying things like: "Hello Mike Four, Hello Mike Four. This is Seagull speaking. Can you send us two more flame throwers? There are snipers in the windmill at the crossroads. Over."

"But at a quarter past ten," said the intelligence officer at Second Corps, "all the radio sets went mad with something different: 'Hello Command, Hello Command, this is Bluebird—or Sunfish—or Water Rat or Film Star.' That is, the Chaudière or the Can Scots or the Queen's Own or the Fort Garry Horse. 'Is it true? Is it true?'

And the word came back that it was true. No more attacks. No more guns. No more appalling splitting mornings. No more of the monstrous cannonade under which, so often, they'd gone forward with the blood pounding in their veins. And then, in a flash, silence! No more challenges in the dark. No more snipers' bullets in the dawn light. No more burial parties in the drifting smoke. No more jeep ambulances bumping down the tank tracks in the cratered roads. No more shouts of frenzy or pain. No more attacks. An enormous silence hung upon the cool spring night of Friday, May 4th. No more guns.

That was the story of how the news had come to the whole 2nd Corps front. Ouimet's broadcast told how it was received by the Chaudière as they stood by to put in an attack.

We had dinner, we chatted about this and everything. I told Colonel Taschereau what I had seen on the American and Russian fronts only a few days before. Then he retired for an hour. The brigadier still wasn't back from his parleys in Aurich. A little after 8:30 Colonel Taschereau came out of his room and said: 'Well, boys, Ouimet was right. The ceasefire is scheduled for eight o'clock tomorrow morning." Most of the officers and men around could hardly believe it. One soldier dashed out of the house and ran to the road. The Seventh Brigade was just passing through on its way into Aurich. "The war is over," he shouted. "This fellow in the carrier," he told me later, "looked at me as if I wasn't sober."

The colonel had the only three bottles of champagne in his headquarters brought in. He held his glass and instead of drinking to victory, as we expected, he turned around to his officers and said: "I drink to Major Rochon, the best soldier in the battalion," and tears came to his eyes as he thought of this youthful company commander who had given his life ten days before. The officers remained silent—tears came to their eyes as well. On the eve of victory, in the forward areas, soldiers thought of other soldiers, those who were gone, who were missing. Of course they were happy, but the gathering never took the form of a hilarious party. Then and there one could sense, once again, the strength of friendships born in battle.

The colonel said: "How I wish he could be with us. . . ."

An officer muttered, as if to himself: "It's a strange feeling. But it's something to be able to realize that it's over, and that one has survived."

A soldier commented: "Tomorrow, for the first time, I'll be able to sit down in a chair and enjoy it. I won't feel restless any more. I'll look forward to the next day and not with the idea that I might get it."

"Colonel," another officer said, "can I command one of the detachments to the victory parade in Paris?"

"As far as I'm concerned," another fellow said, "I'm not so happy. It means that we'll be back to spit and polish. I'll have to wear a tie, I'll have to be clean shaven early every morning. I'll have to get my hair cut once a month, and perhaps more often. My uniform will need pressing, my boots will have to be spotless and shining. Somehow I think combat duty had its good points."

The O.C. was still thoughtful. After a minute or two he smiled broadly. "Do you know what I'm thinking about?" he explained. "I'm thinking about my batman, in Halifax, on September 1st, 1939. How he walked into my room that morning with a terrific grin to tell me that at last war was declared. Yes, that was nearly six years ago!"

We talked and drank until well into the night. Some of the officers were talking of the future. "Right now," they said, "we've got some work on our hands. Turning this battalion from a unit of rugged individuals to a group of well-dressed and precise soldiers."

"That's until we go home," one of them remarked.

"And then Burma," said someone jokingly.

"Why not?" they chorused. "The Americans came to help us."

At dawn I took the road back to camp. It was cold. The rain never stopped until we were well away. We went through a series of small towns and villages—German. At this early hour, some of the citizens were already queuing up at the food stores—they must have known about the capitulation of their armies on the 21st Army Group front. But they never showed it. Then we came into Holland again. The

tri-coloured flags of the Netherlands and the flag of the House of
Orange were all out. Children wore gaily coloured headdresses and
waved at us as we went by, and cheered. It was a great day for the
Netherlands, not only for the victory of some of their allies, but the
day of liberation for still the greatest proportion of their inhabitants.

Somehow the sixth of June seemed so far away, passed so long
ago. But this is how the French-speaking troops of Canada had celebrated the news on their front. In a calm, subdued fashion these
hardy veterans of Normandy, the Scheldt, and the Battle of the Rhine,
had thought more of their fallen comrades than of themselves. "They're
the bravest bunch of men I've ever met," had been Brigadier Roberts'
own words.

Halton had got back to camp on that cool spring night and
sat down at his typewriter.

"The German war," he wrote, "is rushing to its close. But
'rushing' is hardly the right word when every moment is too
long."

He had got as far as that when Lt. Colonel Gilchrist, the
same Bill Gilchrist who had welcomed Peter Stursberg to the
fireworks on the night that Italy was invaded, came up to him
and told him of the German surrender to Montgomery. So he
had to start again.

"The German war is over," he wrote this time. And much
more. The next day he was broadcasting:

During long weary years, and during hours that seemed like years,
one sometimes wondered if the carnival of death wasn't a nightmare
from which one would happily awake. And now that the nightmare
is over, one has to wonder if it isn't a pleasant dream from which
we shall wake to find the usual mad mornings of blood and death.
Today the sun rises as it hasn't risen for nearly six years, and soldiers
I have talked to don't quite know what to do about it. They shave
and have breakfast. They clean their guns. They try to brush the mud
off their clothes. They ask if there is any mail. After all, the've lived
strange, dangerous lives. It's hard to believe that no shells will come
screaming over. It's hard to believe that if they stand up in the open
nobody will shoot at them. Death has walked at their side. It's hard
to believe, for a day or two, that the nightmare is over and they can
drink the wine of life.

The wholesale surrender to Field Marshal Montgomery on

May 4 was followed the next day by the surrender of the German commander in Holland to General Foulkes, commanding the 1st Canadian Corps. Halton and Ouimet, joined now by Paul Barette, were watchers. "The Canadians," Halton broadcast,

have helped to free many countries, and shed much of their choicest blood, and raised themselves in the eyes of the world to the status of a great nation. And the climax of that came yesterday, in the wrecked and desolate little Dutch town of Wageningen, when a Canadian corps commander took the surrender of General von Blaskowitz and the 120,000 Germans of his Holland command, and so liberated Holland at last. We stood at the barrier separating the Canadian Army from the Germans. The barrier was one string of wide tape, the kind we used to mark a passage through a minefield during an attack. When I got there I saw at least two hundred big trucks of the British 49th Division, which is part of First Canadian Corps. I saw them rolling across the dividing tape, carrying food for the Dutch people. Carrying it by arrangement.

Then I saw a small car coming along toward us. It was a shabby German Volkswagen, the equivalent of our jeep. In it were the driver and two German officers—a general and a sabre-scarred colonel who was his interpreter. They were received formally and coldly by Lieutenant-General Charles Foulkes, commanding the First Canadian Corps. With him was Prince Bernhardt of Holland, representing the Dutch government. General Foulkes led the German general into the littered and broken bar of a ruined hotel to hear his terms. The war correspondents present were invited to come in and listen. The German general wore a black leather coat and a shabby big cape. He was a red-faced, brutish looking man. When he saw us he lifted his arm in the Nazi salute, but except for that, he was submissive, even abject, the very picture of a broken man. Sitting there with his head in his hands like the picture of Thiers in front of Bismarck.

So it was over. But even now in the moment of surrender, the Germans were leaving a trail of blood and brutality. Prince Bernhardt told me, with white-hot anger in his voice, that they had killed civilians for rejoicing in the news of the surrender. He said: "When the people heard the news on the radio they ran into the streets to tell their friends. The Germans fired into them. People were killed and wounded in many towns, especially in Rotterdam, Utrecht and Dortrecht." No doubt the Germans will say the people had broken the curfew. The real reason for the massacre, probably, is that they were afraid. None the less, it was an atrocity.

That broadcast of Halton's contained a strange footnote to the myth of the Berchtesgaden Redoubt.

"Prince Bernhardt told me," he said,

that Hitler and Goebbels and the other leaders of the criminal Nazi camarilla were not really dead. He said: "I definitely believe that they intend to foster a new German myth—that Hitler is working underground and will come forward to lead a new German resurgence when the right hour strikes."

That right hour seemed pretty remote now, with a hundred and twenty thousand Germans laying down their arms in an almost hysterical surrender, begging us as von Blaskowitz did to protect them from the angry Dutch. It was pretty nice to see that it was the First Canadian Corps which took the surrender of all those Germans. For a year and a half these men had fought in Italy, and sometimes it seemed that there would be no end. And now, when the Canadians were not there, the Germans had surrendered—a million of them—in Italy. That is why we're glad that it was the First Canadian Corps which took the surrender in Holland and received the freedom of Holland for ever more.

Lloyd Moore and Fred McCord had a triumphal and almost royal progress of their own as liberators. They had started out in one of the vans for a sweep down the coast of northern Holland, their idea being to make a record in sound of the jubilation of the towns and cities they passed through. They had to give up the attempt and be content with flowers and embraces. After the first few hundred small boys had swarmed over and through the van, they hadn't a microphone cord left intact. So they went back to the press camp and the job of recording victory messages from various high personages.

There was much more. The formality of the final surrender at Rheims, V-E Day in London, the victory parades in Berlin, and a continuing celebration in the liberated countries. The flow of transmissions across the Atlantic went on steadily for months. In the United Kingdom there was a job to be done in the setting up, with the help of the BBC, of a Canadian Forces Network of low power stations to serve the Canadians in England awaiting repatriation.

We came home, most of us, by ones and twos. Marcel went on special assignment to Paris before returning home to resume a career which led to a CBC vice-presidency. Matt stayed on as the CBC European correspondent, worked with the BBC on some of their great documentaries, wrote, and continued to cover himself with distinction until his death in 1956. Lloyd Moore had the job of collecting the hard-worked equipment and shipping back to Canada all of it that was useful. But it was all postlude. The job that Bob Bowman and Arthur Holmes had begun when they started up their recording gear on board the *Aquitania* was done when Marcel Ouimet joined the officers of the Chaudière in a drink instead of going into an attack with them; and when Matt Halton wrote: "The German war is over."

The Overseas Unit had had no formal inception and it had no formal end. If anyone had thought its efforts required an epilogue, he might have chosen one of the spate of broadcasts Matt Halton made in the two days after the shooting stopped:

"Today the world is happy. Ten million men pinch themselves and feel that they're still alive and will soon be lying on the lawn listening to their wives and babies."

Then he quoted a verse from John McCrae:

"If ye break faith with us who die
"We shall not sleep, though poppies grow
"In Flanders fields."
"And now," Halton said,

not only in Flanders fields. I've seen them—at Regalbuto and Agira in Sicily, and up the length of Italy. At Potenza and Campobasso— I've seen them there. On the Sangro River and on the Moro River— I've seen them there. At Ortona, in the bloody shell holes of the Gothic Line and the Hitler Line, and in the outskirts of dreaming Florence. In Normandy, at Carpiquet. The wide fields were red with blood and poppies on that morning of July 4 at Carpiquet. In France, Belgium, Holland, Germany, Regalbuto, Moro River, Carpiquet and the appalling hill at Kappelen, the sun shines now. But remember these names, Canada, because they're written on your heart.

INDEX OF PERSONS NAMED